Simpson on Second-hand Boats

Simpson on Second-hand Boats

Andrew Simpson

WATERLINE

Published by Waterline Books
an imprint of Airlife Publishing Ltd
101 Longden Rd, Shrewsbury, England

© Andrew Simpson1993

ISBN 1 85310 371 3

A Sheerstrake production.

A CIP catalogue record of this book
is available from the British Library

Contents

1	Introduction	5
2	Astern	6
3	Finding	10
4	Research	17
5	Choosing	24
6	Seeing	32
7	Timber	37
8	Glass Reinforced Plastic (GRP)	49
9	Steel	66
10	Aloft — Spars and Rigging	70
11	Sail Tales	81
12	Deck Hardware	84

13	The Nuts & Bolts	88
14	Sparks — The Electrics & Electronics	95
15	The Comforts of Home	99
16	Buying	101
17	Selling	110
Index		117

1 Introduction

Apart perhaps from raising children or running a string of racehorses, there are few pursuits in life more costly than owning a yacht. It's like being stricken by some desperate and debilitating disease of the wallet, for which there is no known cure. And yet, curiously, most yachtsmen bear their suffering with an almost manic joy — the kind of daftness which in any right-minded society would have you instantly consigned to the funny farm. There is a conflict between logic and a lust for life which afflicts all yachtsmen — and logic rarely wins.

But crazy isn't necessarily stupid. Boat ownership may be an expensive game but that doesn't mean you should wantonly toss your money away. Even when being extravagant, it makes sense to spend as wisely as possible — if only to help quell those feelings of guilt.

Obviously by far the most expensive item of equipment is the boat itself. And, as is the way of such things, second-hand usually costs less than new. Much of this book is about buying a second-hand boat — how to find it, what to look for, and how to deal with the negotiations.

In a later section we deal with selling — the other side of the same coin. Buyers and sellers are partners in the same mad dance. To perform nimbly in one role it pays to understand the other.

Although this book may seem to have been written predominantly from the stand-point of sailing, rather than power boats, many of·the comments are relevant to both. This apparent chauvinism on my part was done not from any prejudice or partiality but simply to make the writing less congested with superfluous qualifications — rather in the same sense that I have used 'he' or 'his' when it could also be 'she' or 'hers'. After all, a modern sailing boat is in many ways the same as a power boat with the added complication of all that knitting aloft. Therefore, if I talk of 'yacht' or 'boat' or 'vessel' or whatever, unless the distinction is obvious from the context, then I could mean a boat of any sort.

And this is by no means an exhaustive treatise covering all aspects of this subject, but more a rag-bag of hints and insights which I hope will be useful. Many of the comments would sit equally comfortably in different sections and, therefore, may not be where you might expect to find them.

This is therefore a book to be delved into rather than assiduously studied.

2 Astern _____

Boatbuilding has always been a high risk business, but never more so than over the past few years. Of the firms that were active two decades ago, only a handful remain. Some well-known names have survived but, of these, only a tiny number are under the same ownership. The others have foundered in the fiercer ebbs of commercial fortune.

In attributing blame it's tempting to point accusing fingers at the swoops and plunges of our economy. But this would be a simplistic explanation, glossing over other important factors.

Sailing as we know it today sprang from the post-war austerity of the fifties. Before then, *yachting* (the word 'sailing' seems somehow insufficient) had been a predominantly snooty pursuit, enjoyed by gents with deeper than average pockets. Even by the standards of the day, yachts were expensive. In tilted sheds around our coast, craftsmen and their scurrying apprentices hewed timber from the rough, shaped it with adzes, bent it in dragon-breathed steam boxes, and joined it all together with thousands of rivets and roves. Of course, this was a horrendously laborious process, but no one was in a hurry. It was generally accepted that these grand and individual creations would take a gang of men several months to build. The most prestigious boatyards maintained waiting lists, turning away custom which was not to their taste. By and large their clients were content with this arrangement and so, naturally enough, were the builders. Although in terms of actual launchings their out-put was low, the commodity they were producing was sufficiently valuable to sustain their turnover.

But, then along came Hitler and spoiled it all for everyone. Yachting was all but suspended. Many shipwrights were soon conscripted into the services, and the ones who remained at their benches were obliged to turn their skills to building ships of war. Where once graceful yachts had been crafted, the bluffer forms of patrol boats and ships' lifeboats took shape. Urgency nudged aside the more comfortable rhythms of peace. Outsiders — including many women — were brought in to replace those who had gone off to fight. Utility, economy, and efficiency of production became the new order.

Six years later, with hostilities ended and Europe in tatters, the world had changed irrevocably. There had been considerable erosion to old privileges. Many of the pre-war yachts had been stripped for their vital materials, had been destroyed entirely, or had fallen into such disrepair that they were no longer serviceable. And, on a human level, there was a bruised generation desperate to forget recent horrors. A different class of person was eager to go sailing, and there was a different type of boatbuilder already in place to give him what he wanted.

Designers such as Robert Tucker and Maurice Griffiths had sensed this wind-shift and knew exactly what was needed — smallish cheap and cheerful yachts that could be series built by an industry now well-accustomed to *factory* techniques.

The obvious material of the moment was plywood. It had appeared on the marine scene around 1939 and had been further developed during the war years. It was ideal for systemised construction. Large panels could be assembled by relatively unskilled labour, using inexpensive hand tools and jigs. And, with supplies from overseas still uncertain, it wasn't even necessary to be fussy about the choice of woods. Timber previously considered unsuited for boatbuilding could be peeled into veneers and used in its manufacture. There were limitations on the kind of shapes that could be constructed with sheet ply (compound curves are virtually impossible), but this was a small price to pay when set against the ease and speed of production.

Fanned by the availability of these newly accessible boats, the sport of sailing proliferated. Our harbours and creeks became dotted with hundreds of small craft. Summer days, once tranquil, were now alive with the flapping of sails and the splutter of outboard motors. Many of the older hands in the yachting establishment became distinctly purple of face at this rude invasion of their territory by the commoner man, but there was no restraining what had become an unstoppable recreational explosion.

Two classic second-hand boats. A wooden Folkboat and a GRP Nicholson 32 in adjacent berths.

The small family yacht was here to stay but, unfortunately, at first not for very long. For cheap and cheerful is also often short-lived, and so it was with those early boats. Crude construction techniques and lack of proper protection (especially to panel edges where water could penetrate) meant that rot and delamination were a constant blight. And the very designs themselves, with their hidden corners and unvented spaces, were an invitation to decay.

Anyway, our new brand of yachtsman was already getting bored with the Spartan accommodation offered by these pocket craft. A sufficient number of ritzier yachts were around to provide invidious contrasts. Hardly surprisingly, ambitions grew with experience and burgeoning prosperity. Four damp berths and a bucket-and-chuck-it loo may have been tolerable for starters but, with money more plentiful, it was obvious that the industry was going to have to do better.

And it did. Towards the end of the fifties, fibreglass made an appearance. By the mid-sixties, it had really taken hold. Sailing was ripe for this new wonder material and, after some initial suspicions, it was greeted rapturously. 'Maintenance

8

free!' howled the advertisements. 'Throw away your paint brushes!' The hour of the everlasting boat was at hand.

Well, now we all know this was nonsense but, at the time, it was seductive stuff. I can remember gazing admiringly at the gunter-rigged Westerly 22 when it first sailed into my view. With a scraper in my hand and my skin stinging with paint stripper, I probably hid my envy behind affectations of scorn, but age and honesty now force me to admit that I was pretty impressed. Those smooth curves and virgin pure topsides were as alluring to me as a Siren's call. As soon as my wallet allowed I became an ardent convert.

Of course, now we know that glass reinforced plastic boats are not without their problems. But, nevertheless, they have often proved more durable than the firms that built them. This is more than just an ironic observation; it's also a good part of the cause of the decline in boatbuilding. For, whilst the plywood boats of the fifties and early sixties have disappeared almost entirely, by far the majority of *all* the GRP boats ever built are still in existence. In providing boats which wore out only very slowly, the boatbuilding industry progressively diminished its own market.

Other industries have faced similar problems. There is always commercial embarrassment in having a product hang around long enough to haunt its creators. To overcome this, many have resorted to that legitimised skullduggery coyly known as 'planned obsolescence'. But having an object fall apart in tune with some manufacturer's marketing schedule might be tolerable for, say, washing machines or motor cars, but is hardly good news for boats which are literally life-supporting. We are already seeing signs of this in some modern craft, and it's a depressing and chilling development.

Springing directly from this unease is the growing feeling amongst informed sailors that *older might actually be better*. Or, to put it another way, that in opting to buy second-hand you would really be settling for more not less. With certain qualifications, I agree with these sentiments, and would put my money on a good quality mid-seventies yacht — a Nicholson 32, for example — outliving many of the 'plastic fantastics' being built today.

So, what of the future? The saying of sooths was never my strong point, but I believe that there might only be room for a few large manufacturers. These would satisfy the ongoing need for new production models — topping up, as required, the huge pool of second-hand boats. Smaller firms will deal with specialised needs — including racing yachts, serious ocean cruisers, vintage replicas, and multihulls. For the other yards there will be the enormous task of repairing and maintaining the existing fleet — a fleet whose replacement rate is likely to be much, much slower than we have seen in the past.

Already, for most yachtsmen in search of a boat, the first place to look would be the second-hand market. Every conceivable type of boat is on offer somewhere — at sizes and prices to suit almost everyone's pocket. It's very difficult to see when it might ever be otherwise.

3 Finding

Location

By their very nature, boats are mobile objects. And, if you want to buy one, tracking it down can be a daunting task, in many ways even more frustrating than buying a house. No one who wants to live in Brighton, for instance, would dream of traipsing off to Falmouth because a house attracts him; but that's exactly what might be required if you are hot on the trail of the ideal boat.

The casting of such a wide net obviously increases choice, but can also exact a cruel price in terms of worn tyres and frayed nerves. For those who want to maximise effect and minimise pain, it pays to box clever. Some forethought and planning will narrow the search.

The Lay of the Land: Naturally enough, the kind of boats we're interested in tend to congregate along the frilly bits around the edges of our island. Quite obviously, this is where we should concentrate our search.

But our coastline is far from uniform. Indeed it is wonderful in its variety. All of our numerous estuaries, sounds, bays and inlets have their own unique topography. Some are wide and shallow, others narrow and deep; some are navigable in all conditions, others can be unenterable at certain states of the

Drying harbours are good places to look for bilge-keelers.

tide or treacherous with the wind from a particular direction. And so it goes on. These physical characteristics can impose limitations on the boats they harbour, attracting those that are suited and discouraging — or even barring altogether — those that aren't.

By studying local charts it's often possible to predict with some accuracy the sort of boats you will find in any specific location — even if that prediction is that *all* types could be represented there.

Depth of available water exerts the most compelling influence. And by that, of course, we mean the *minimum* depth of water. As examples, let's consider three typical but dissimilar localities, representative of other ports around our coast:

Lyme Regis: A totally drying harbour which can be entered by almost any boat at high water but is wall-to-wall sand and mud with the plug pulled out. Lyme would be the stuff of nightmares for the owner of, say, a Sigma 33, but would be ideal for a bilge-keeled Westerly Centaur or a small long keeled yacht which could take the ground when fitted with legs. Definitely no place to look for a fin-keeler.

The Hamble River: Almost the opposite. Here nearly every mooring is in deep water and fin-keeled boats of every description abound. Where moorings are concerned, deep is also usually expensive, so most of the bilge-keelers (more so the smaller ones) have left the keelers to it and gone off to seek cheaper berths elsewhere.

Poole Harbour: A large expanse of water offering a range of conditions. Much of the harbour is very shallow — great for power boats, bilge-keelers, centre-boarders, multihulls, and other puddle hoppers — but there are also dredged areas that will accommodate deeper drawing vessels, even up to the size of cross-Channel ro-ro ferries. Almost any type of yacht *could* be found in Poole, but smaller classes will be the most prevalent.

Interestingly, even within harbours like Poole, the principles of topographical selection exist on a localised scale. Access to the various boatyards dotted around the perimeter is, as everywhere else, limited by available water. When laying up for the winter the larger boats will gravitate towards those yards with superior access (and often tariffs to match), whilst nimbler craft will skip ashore elsewhere. Drive from boatyard to boatyard and, to a large extent, you will find like conveniently clustered with like.

The Swank Factor: Perhaps as influential as the shape of the putty — and in many ways closely related.

Market forces can be assumed to prevail. Good quality moorings in desirable locations will command the highest prices. In Monte Carlo, for instance, the annual cost of a berthing a gin palace would buy outright a very nice modern yacht. Such places have inevitably become reservations for the super-rich; the hoi polloi being excluded by their inability to pay. In Britain we don't have quite such grotesque extremes, but there are certainly some areas which are conspicuously nobbier than others. Take a trip around the Solent, note its contrasts, and you'll see exactly what I mean.

Rich men can afford fancier toys, so expensive places are where to look for expensive boats. And vice-versa.

Marinas: These too vary in salubriousness. Although none have ever been particularly bashful about charging top dollar for the services they provide, some have recently become very greedy.

Berthing fees are usually calculated by length. Most marinas impose a minimum charge — often based on a 26' (8m) LOA — which will be levied even if the boat is shorter. Therefore, do not expect to find many tiny boats lying alongside in marinas — though they could be stored ashore there for the winter lay-up.

The Global Marketplace: Distant parts are often the graveyards of dreams. Go to places like Gibraltar, the Canaries, Barbados, or Hawaii, and you will see yachts abandoned by their disillusioned owners. Of course the mileage required to search in these areas is prodigious but, especially for the larger boats, it can prove worth the effort.

I was in Vigo a couple of years ago, sitting out a gale whilst on passage to the Med. Perched in the companionway, I was gazing morosely out over the rain-slashed harbour when I observed a Twister coming in through the entrance. The headsail lay bunched on the foredeck, but the mainsail, deeply reefed, was still set. At the tiller was an elderly man. Wrapped around his head was what appeared to be a scarlet bandanna. His eyes were fixed determinedly upon a vacant berth some distance from my own.

Without fenders the little boat crashed at some speed into the berth. I could see the helmsman reel at the impact, and then he was scrambling ashore to make fast the lines.

What happened next was unexpected. By now I had shrugged on my oilskins and was on my way to offer assistance. I was in my own cockpit, just about to step onto the pontoon when I saw a duffle bag come flying out of the Twister's open companionway. This was followed almost immediately by a dumpy little woman of roughly the same age as the man. Seizing the bag, she leapt ashore and, without word or glance at the poor fellow now wrestling to hand the mainsail, stomped purposefully off down the jetty.

Later, large whiskies in hand and after I had re-bandaged a nasty cut on his head, I found out from the man — the husband, as it turned out — what had happened. In anticipation of their retirement, they had bought the boat some years earlier, at first restricting their cruising to the area around Falmouth. Finally, with work behind them and their affairs in order, they had set off on what was to have been an indefinite world cruise. Off Brest in thick fog they had been narrowly missed by a large ship. Then they had been becalmed for six days, unable to run the engine because, when they tried to start it, the wiring loom had burst into flames.

'And after the fire and the calm', he told me dolefully, 'of course there *had* to be the bloody gale. Knocked down twice we were. Doris was on the loo the second time.' He paused to savour both the whisky and the memory. Gingerly, he fingered the fresh bandage. 'Then we gybed all standing and the boom got me. Doris was at the helm for nearly twenty hours before I was in any state.'

And that's the way it sadly ended. I heard later that their boat had been put on the market, and, after very little interest from anybody in Vigo, had eventually been sold for a song to an American who was passing through. So, a shattered dream and a dented marriage — and for a total stranger a very nice boat at a nicer price.

But at least the boat got a second chance.

Going for brokers

Yacht brokers are the marriage bureaux of the yachting world. They operate in much the same way as estate agents, selling boats on a commission basis on behalf of their owners. For the purchaser they provide the nearest thing to one-stop shopping that there is.

Yacht brokers, in their various degrees of suavity, tend to reflect the general tone of the areas in which they work. Exalted places attract lofty brokerage firms, and so on. One yachtsman I know claims he can judge the price of the boats by the depth of the carpet pile.

Many brokers operate over a large territory — nationally, or even internationally — and may list almost any kind of yacht. Others restrict their activities to a designated area — perhaps just within the confines of a single marina — and will therefore be limited by the types of boat found there.

The most reputable yacht brokers in the UK belong to the *Association of Brokers and Yacht Agents* (ABYA), associated in turn with the *Yacht Brokers and Designers and Surveyors Association* (YBDSA). It pays to check. Members must comply with a strictly enforced Code of Practice, and must carry insurance to protect clients against any losses caused by their negligence or malpractice. If a brokerage firm is not a member, then there might be a very good reason, of which you should be wary.

Some Brokers Are Specialists: It's important to contact the right man. There's no point in talking to a classic boat specialist if you've actually set your heart on a go-fast racing machine.

Review the ads in the yachting magazines and see who handles what.

Be As Specific As You Can: Brokers are simple fellows and easily confused. A broker friend of mine reported a recent telephone conversation, which went something like this:

'Hullo. I would like to buy a yacht.'

'A yacht? Well, yes, I think we can help you there.' The tone of the broker is warm and encouraging. He is well versed in dealing with the insane. He reaches for his pencil. 'Now, sir, what sort of yacht do you have in mind?'

'What sort of yachts do you have?'

Our broker blinks. His eyes flick to the wall, where hundreds of photographs are pinned. He coughs. 'A fair selection, sir. We are talking about a sailing boat, I take it?'

'Of course. Didn't I say "yacht"?'

'Er...yes. Actually, we do have motor yachts as well, but never mind. Size?'

'Pardon?'

'How big a yacht do you want?'

The telephone is mute for some seconds. At the customer's end there is much knitting of brows. 'At least thirty feet or so...maybe forty. It depends on how large a yacht I can afford.'

'Ahah!' exclaims the yacht broker, his face now alight with interest. Nothing cheers brokers up more than getting round to the money. 'And how much is that, pray?'

'Well, I'm not exactly certain at the moment. I'd take out a second mortgage on the house, of course, but prices are a bit depressed right now. But I do have a few quid in the building society. And there's the wife's brother Denis. He said he'd toss in a couple of thou if he could use the yacht when we didn't need it.'

'Yes...I see,' said the broker, not seeing at all. 'But perhaps an indication?'

Another long pause. 'Nine or ten thousand?' suggested the customer tentatively.

On the top sheet of his pad, our broker has doodled a dagger. Sadly, he rips the page off, screws it into a ball, and tosses it into the bin.

This sort of approach plainly won't do. No yacht broker is going to be whipped into action by such a woolly grasp of the matter. The spread in boat size is too wide — covering umpteen different classes and tens of thousands of pounds in price. Also, the customer has clearly signalled that any boat within those size limits will probably be beyond his means, anyway. Our yacht broker, being a commercially minded chap at heart, will be convinced he's wasting his time. As soon as he hangs up, he's certain to return to his crossword.

As covered in a previous section, it's vital to do your homework first. When you talk to a yacht broker he will want to know at least the following:

1)   Precisely what sort of vessel you require. If not by specific class (or selection of classes if you have alternatives in mind) then at least defined as tightly as possible in terms of size, accommodation, keel type, and rig preferred.

2)   Your absolute price limit. The word 'absolute' is important here. Yacht brokers are great ones for deciding you can afford more than you think you can. Ask about fifteen-thousand-pound boats and you're suddenly shown some at twenty. Tell the man exactly how much you can afford and impress upon him that you understand your own financial circumstances better than he does.

And be reasonable. If your expectations are unrealistic, the broker will have no chance of fulfilling them. He can only offer you what is available under the current market conditions.

If you are generally floundering and do not know what you are looking for, then refer to the next chapter on *Research*. In my opinion, yacht brokers are not always the best people to go to for guidance. There are better ways to crystalise your thinking. No matter how scrupulous the broker may be, the incentive for him to complete a sale is a powerful one. His position is by no means unbiased. You might find yourself steered towards a boat which is not necessarily perfect for you, but simply the most suitable one the broker can offer at the moment.

Going it alone
Classified Advertisements: The small ads at the back of the yachting magazines provide fascinating catalogues of boats for sale. Of course, because of the time elapsed between placement and printing, these will all be a few weeks out of date. But it's still worth phoning around.

As we cover in the next chapter, different magazines have different editorial textures, and this is mirrored in the type of yachts advertised. Read them all avidly, but expect better results from the magazine which most closely matches your own tastes.

The Pre-emptive Approach: Many of the best deals are struck before a boat ever comes onto the open market. There are scores of owners out there on the verge of selling their boats. An approach from you could tip them over the brink.

Circulate the yacht clubs. Most will cheerfully post a small legibly written notice on their boards. Again, be precise in your requirements but make no reference to price; that can be the subject of less public discussion later.

The 'If-you-ever-think-of-selling' approach has worked very well for one man I know. To my knowledge he has bought at least four boats that way over the years. If he sees a yacht that interests him, he simply hails the owner and leaves his card. Far from being offended, most are usually flattered. His proudest boast is having spotted, hailed, boarded, caroused on, and bought a boat during the course of a single afternoon.

4 Research_____

I have yet to meet a yachtsman who didn't spend hours reading up on the subject. This is easily understandable in Britain where, with the boat laid up during the winter, severe sensory deprivation demands compensatory outlets; but I've also noticed the phenomena in such idyllic places as the Caribbean. Here there is no excuse. The man cruising the tropics whilst reading about another man cruising the tropics, is simply displaying another conspicuous symptom of our common affliction.

Personally, I've always found reading a particularly effective way of absorbing information. Unlike conversation, where you are bound by polite social restraints, you can react openly (though of course impotently) to opinions you disagree with. No writer is going to be offended by an unheard hoot of disparagement, or a distantly curled lip. And there are other advantages, too: you can flip through the boring bits; you can terminate the encounter by simply closing the pages; and you really can crawl into bed with someone just for his mind.

We Brits are blessed with better than average access to maritime reading material. Apart from the stream of books which are published, we are treated monthly to a feast of magazines which rank amongst the very best in the world.

For the newcomer to sailing, a rich harvest of information can be gleaned from their pages. For the prospective purchaser, anxious to develop a sense for what may or may not suit him, there is no better place in which to forage. Boat tests furnish comparative assessments of the virtues (or otherwise) of different designs; cruising yarns give the personal angle — often more informative than dryly presented facts; and specialists in all manner of technically related subjects trot out their expertise for your amusement and education.

Of course boating magazines are not exactly alike in their editorial texture. Although there is considerable overlap, each is pitched at a slightly different market, and might express contradictory views on the same topic. For instance, a racing journalist could damn a boat for its docility — and another writing on cruising might heap praise upon that same boat for precisely the same reason.

It would be useful to read them *all*, if practicable, no matter how out of step they may be with your own thoughts. In the formation of opinion, ideally there should be some cross-fertilisation of ideas. Even an article that leaves you howling with derision will have caused you to pause for a moment to think about it.

Boating Magazines — Sail

Yachting World: Circulation 31,700. Once this was acknowledged as the 'establishment' monthly, aimed very much towards the affluent end of the market. Although today still covering much of the same hallowed ground, there has recently been a discernible shift towards racing and other aspects of high performance sailing. This is the magazine to read if you want to know what happened at Cowes Week, or learn about the latest maxi to be launched.

Yachting World holds regular rallies, where boats of similar size and type (and by no means only the big ones) can be directly compared. Advertising is generally for the more expensive yachts, but I imagine the management would like to erode this rather rarefied reputation and appeal to a broader church.

Yachts and Yachting: Circulation 22,500. A fortnightly magazine, again with a distinct performance bias. *Yachts and Yachting* regularly dips its toes into big boat racing, but is more authentically the journal of the smaller racing keelboat and dinghy sailing fraternity. The advertising reflects this interest.

Yachting Monthly: Circulation 51,000. The cruising sailors' magazine. The ultimate browse for those whose lust is mainly of the wander variety. Editorial content is a rich mix of 'how to' and 'where to', with cruising yarns a'plenty from outside contributors. Such luminaries as Maurice Griffith and Des Sleighthome are numbered amongst previous editors, so it is hardly surprising that *Yachting Monthly* speaks with an authoritative voice. Densely packed with advertising on all manner of boats and equipment.

Multihull International: Circulation 8,500 by subscription. The only monthly multihull journal available. The specialisation places predictable limits on editorial scope, but the articles will be of undoubted interest to devotees, or those with an emergent interest in multihulls. The obvious first choice for multihull advertisements.

Power

Motor Boats Monthly: Circulation 18,500. A monthly glossy covering all aspects of power boating. Generally informative and well presented with heavy advertising for all types of motor craft.

Both

Practical Boat Owner: Circulation 70,000. Britain's biggest selling yachting magazine — known almost universally as *PBO*. This is a middle-of the road monthly with strong DIY tendencies. Lately, *PBO* has somewhat shaken off its '*how-to-make-an-anchor-light-out-of-a-fish-paste-jar*' image, but it still leans cheerfully towards budget boating with a self-help approach. There is some power boating coverage, but mainly this is a sailing magazine. Advertising is broadly based, but thinner for the more up-market yachts.

Motor Boat & Yachting: Circulation 35,000. Although to some extent this monthly straddles the line between sail and power, its principal interest centres firmly on motor cruising. The advertising is similarly biased.

Classic Boat: Circulation 19,400. The title is self-explanatory. This monthly covers the world of classic type yachts — both sail and power, genuinely old or replicas. Because such craft are usually (but not always) one-offs, this is not a notably fruitful fount of information on 'class' boats, but the compensations in sheer reading pleasure make it worth the effort. The advertising represents an absorbing glance astern at our yachting past.

Boat Mart International: Concerned mainly with small, trailerable power boats and their accessories, but also with some sailing content. In my opinion, not much of a read, but you do sometimes see something interesting amongst the advertisements.

Back Issues: Like most committed yachtsmen, my house has become a repository for hundreds of old yachting magazines. Try as I might, I simply can't bring myself to throw them away. Dusty stacks stand in various parts of the house. There are more in the loo, still more in the attic, and even the boat floats an inch or so lower than it should with those glossy wads stowed in various lockers. Somewhere in my head there is a vague but surprisingly effective indexing system that seems to know approximately where to look when I need to refer to something. Details of a Swanage Sludge Skimmer, circa 1960? It's up the ladder, turn right at the cistern, and it's halfway down the big pile under the eaves. This is my justification for keeping the darned things.

Back issues, if you can find them, are always a wonderful aid to research. Some folk will even stoop to theft to obtain a particular copy. A man I know was so wracked with guilt after snaffling one from a doctor's waiting room that he felt moved to donate a tenner to the Heart Foundation. It was probably well worth the money all round.

The trial sail
When it comes to learning about boats, nothing beats hands-on experience. A few hours afloat in the yacht of your choice can either endorse or puncture your dreams.

In the late seventies, I was living and working in Texas. Amongst my other design commissions was a fifty-footer for a millionaire oil man. I had barely finished the provisional sketches when he 'phoned me up and told me to place the project on hold. Apparently a boatbuilder in Florida had just brought out a new production mega-yacht which he had exhibited at a recent boat show. This had really taken my oil man's fancy.

'See what sort of deal I can strike, cash in hand,' he told me.

'No trial sail?' I prompted.

'Think it's necessary?'

'Sure do', I told him, displaying my full mastery of the American language, and went on to explain why.

Anyway, the upshot of all this was that my oil man and his brand new girlfriend arranged to fly out in his helicopter to a rig parked some fifty miles offshore in the Gulf of Mexico. There he would join the demonstrator which would sail out from Galveston to rendezvous with him. A date was set.

Unfortunately, the date was also set for the passage of a particularly nasty cold front (known locally and with some aptness as a 'norther') to come whipping down from upstate to trounce them. Demonstrator, crew, oil man, and unsuspecting girlfriend were comprehensively tumbled about in a boat which all but totally came apart. Bulkheads and much of the other interior structure came loose, the oven tore free from its gimbals and bounced around the cabin a bit (doing no good at all to the fancy joinery work, you may imagine), the loo holding tank partially discharged its contents at extreme angles of heel, and even the celebratory champagne popped its corks in disgust.

Needless to say, the builders didn't complete the sale. And, it's sad to relate, neither did I. As aversion therapy went, that short trip proved powerful medicine. My oil man took himself, and his money away from the coast, and bought a ranch on which to raise Texas longhorn cattle. Far from being grateful for my advice, he seemed to hold me personally responsible for his ordeal.

Actually, he was a lucky man. He had learned a valuable lesson before he had committed himself. If he had gone sailing in a decent boat — even in those conditions — the story might have ended differently. But that was not to be.

Adopt a broad view
Many people come into boat ownership already thoroughly prejudiced. The man who started sailing with a friend, may have been so impressed with his boat (or type of boat) that he is well on his way to making a similar choice himself — regardless of whether or not it would actually suit him best. This tunnel-vision could prevent him making a better choice.

In the days when I was designing and racing multihulls, I regularly astonished confirmed keelboat sailors simply by taking them for a ride on one of my trimarans. It was not the speed that surprised them, but the lack of vices they *assumed* the boat would have. Opinions are often formed in ignorance, and then transmitted to others as immutable truths.

As a rider to this, it's worth remembering that every yacht owner has 'the best boat afloat'. Listen in at any yacht club conversation and you can hear the members trying to out-brag each other. When you hear a man praising another man's boat, it's probably worth listening to; when he's talking about his own, then a shovelful of salt may not go amiss.

Flotilla Holidays
A pleasant, convivial, and relatively inexpensive way to expand your experience — often in wonderful surroundings. But you won't find many older yachts. Flotillas are usually slickly run organisations with fleets made up of newly minted models, often of French manufacture. Nonetheless, a wide variety of sizes are on offer, and it's worth looking through the brochures to see if anything interests you. Beware, though — the gleaming flotilla work-horses often have purpose-built layouts fitted into standard hulls; which may differ considerably from the production versions.

Bareboat Charters
Another way to try before you buy. Many charter companies are run on a shoestring, so here you will find older designs — some positively ancient. Indeed, many operators actually *prefer* their boats to be a little long in the tooth, recognising that they will inevitably be knocked about during the course of a season, and believing them to be less fragile than their modern counterparts. Leafing through the yachting magazines' small-ads will tell you what's available.

Put yourself about a bit
Take a stroll through a marina and chat to the people on their boats. Ask questions. Yacht owners are a gregarious breed, usually eager to talk to anyone interested enough to listen. Watch out for the exaggerations...*'Poole to Cherbourg in under six hours, and we hove-to for a while for lunch'*...and you may learn a lot. Listen to the lady of the boat, if she's aboard. Catch her wincing when the old man's in spate, and you'll know you're deep in porky-pie territory.

Some owners are chronically short of crew, and you may even find yourself pressed to go sailing. After the event, offer a realistic contribution towards the fuel, food, and booze and you'll be certain to part friends.

Crewing registers
These are the dating agencies of sailing, pairing short-handed owners with willing bodies in a way which hopefully satisfies all. Crew registers — except for those sometimes maintained by clubs or sailing associations — are usually small commercial

operations which exist by exacting a modest fee for the services they offer.

Typically, an annual payment of about £30 will give you continuously updated names and telephone numbers to contact. Through the wonders of computerisation, these lists are filtered to exclude mutually unacceptable — smokers, yodelling enthusiasts, whatever. It is usually up to you to make the arrangements from then on.

If you are keen to have hands-on experience, and have no better means of arranging it, this could be the way to go. Naturally, if you want to sail a particular model, you must specify it on the registration form, hoping that they have such a boat listed. But even taking pot luck will broaden your experience and help fine-tune your choice.

5 Choosing

So far as buying a boat is concerned, the man who's made his mind up is both fortunate and rare.

It seems such a simple thing to do — mesh requirements with cash availability, stir in a few aesthetic preferences for flavour, and there for all to see is the Perfect Boat For You. But, for most of us, there is often confusion and indecision. The longer we roll around our options, the less confident we are. The floating voter has nothing on the stranded sailor.

Before we even think about specific designs, we should ask ourselves the following questions.

1) How much can I afford?

2) What sort of boat would suit me best within that price bracket?

So, there you are. I should be able to close the chapter with this straightforward advice, but perhaps we should explore these points a little further, touching upon related subjects.

Depth of pocket factor

By far the sternest rein on our ambitions. Although an astonishing number of people believe otherwise, most of us recognise that we cannot spend more than we have in the bank, or can realistically borrow. Determining how much this actually is can be a quenching exercise, but is obviously necessary before there can be any choice of boat.

It would be impertinent of me to suggest how you should go about calculating your own financial ceiling, but I can certainly implore you to do so as accurately and with as little self-deception as possible.

And remember the running costs. Someone once said that buying a boat was like collecting mother and baby from the maternity unit — the ecstasy is astern and the expenses lie ahead.

Bargains are usually anything but

The exceptionally cheap yacht is likely to be worth much *less* than the asking price, not more.

One bright spring day I was sat at my desk when a young couple came into my office. Eagerly they told me they had seen a 'fantastic boat' and wanted my opinion. They described an elderly mahogany on oak motor cruiser, of which I had slight knowledge. The conversation proceeded thus:

'They're only asking five grand, but I think we can knock 'em down to four.'

'Four thousand pounds — for a forty-two footer?' My incredulity was apparent.

The young man grinned happily. 'Of course, it needs a bit of work, but we thought we could do it up ourselves. I've got a GCE in carpentry. We want to live on it for a couple of years, and then take it down to the Med.'

'And I could do all the painting and sewing,' added his girlfriend. 'The upholstery wouldn't be a problem.'

Reluctantly I agreed to have a look at it, and followed them over to a nearby boatyard. As soon as I clapped eyes on the boat, my worst fears were confirmed. Sway-backed and rotten, with grass growing all around her, it was plain she hadn't seen the sea for years. Inside, the stench of decay was everywhere. Leprous varnish hung in black strips from the joinery work. The brass fittings were green with verdigris, the engines solid with rust.

As gently as I could, I told them that this was no dream, but a nightmare. The boat was quite beyond economic repair — even by an enthusiastic couple beavering away in their own time. The 'too-good-to-turn-down' asking price was clearly nothing more than the last twitch of a desperate owner, hopefully trying to salvage a few pounds from an obvious total loss.

Relatively speaking, there is no such thing as a cheap boat. Any yacht selling for five grand, when it should be worth fifty in good nick, actually is probably worth *nothing at all!*

Size and space — the sardine principle

Berths sell — this is the marketing adage that has shaped our boats over the past few years. Large yachts can absorb a fair number of bodies without being overly cramped. But small ones will assume all the charm of an 17th Century slaver if used to capacity.

Below is a table illustrating how boat buyers can be lured. For different sizes of cruising yacht I have shown the number of berth spaces typically offered, the ideal complement, and the realistic maximum crew for anything more than a day's sail.

LOA	Berths offered.	Ideal.	Realistic Max
25' (7.62m)	4–6	2	4
30' (9.14m)	5–8	2	4
35' (10.67m)	6–8	4	6
40' (12.19m)	6–9	4	6
45' (13.72m)	7–10	4	6
50' (15.24m)	8–12	6	8

Recently, I was standing at the yacht club bar when a friend hove into view. Consternation was incised deeply on his brow.

'Anything amiss?' I enquired solicitously.

He skewered me with a thunderous look. 'Off on the next tide and someone's dropped out,' he growled.

'Bad luck,' I replied. 'Left you short-handed, eh?'

'Certainly have — seven bloody berths and only six people to fill 'em! Damned if I know what the world's coming to.'

Now, it's well known that nature abhors a vacuum, but less well known that some boat owners do too.

Personally, I go to sea as much for the solitude as anything else. And, if I can't have solitude, then excellent company is the next best thing. My wife Chele and I compile our guest lists with all the delicacy of society hostesses planning a *soiree.*

Others aren't so fussy. Large Scotsmen, small sailmakers, rampaging students — all manner of peculiar life-forms are crammed aboard to lambast boat, ears, and tender sensibilities alike.

All of this is a circuitous way of saying that there is an inescapable relationship between the size of the boat, the number of the crew, and your capacity to tolerate chumminess. But it is not to say that, just because you have a large boat, you should feel obliged to fill it with people. Two experienced sailors could easily handle a modern fifty-footer, four would make life somewhat easier, and six — perhaps the ideal complement — allows you to organise the watches and other duties in a very agreeable way. As almost any yacht will accommodate at least four, to buy simply on the basis of extra berth space is plainly absurd.

Divide and conquer — the centre cockpit
Another powerful marketing feature — and, in my opinion, in many instances of about as dubious worth as all those spare berths. Although divided accommodation can make sense on the larger yacht — say, above 35' (10.67m) LOA — anything smaller can become intolerably cramped, both below and on deck.

Comfort in the cockpit can also be impaired. To sit directly in the accelerated airflow of the slot, with the foresheets flogging around your ears and the mainsail dripping from above, is not one of life's great pleasures.

The small yacht with aft and main cabins joined by a passageway is a particular nonsense. To sacrifice valuable cockpit locker space for so little gain seems to be just silly.

But separate aft cabins can sometimes be desirable. For years I've argued the case for integrated interior   lay-outs with a couple who own (and think the world of) a centre cockpit thirty-footer. Recently, however, I've met their children, and see that they have a point.

Keels — one or two?
Bilge keelers are a curiously British phenomena. There is very little enthusiasm for them elsewhere.

On the plus side, they draw less water and will take the ground without falling over. On the minus side, they have more wetted surface area and less hydrodynamic efficiency than the equivalent fin keel. Consequently, they will be likely to perform less well in light conditions or when beating to windward. Bilge keelers tend to be rather more prone to structural problems, too. On a drying mooring (especially in soft mud) the keels can get wedged apart, straining their attachments to the hull.

It seems to me that some people opt for bilge keels when they won't benefit from them as much as they think they will. Overall, unless local sailing conditions dictate otherwise, the single keel boat is usually the better choice.

Masts — the more the merrier?
Not on anything much less than 40' (12.19m) LOA, say I.

The principle argument in favour of ketches is:

1) that the sails can be balanced better, and:

2) that dividing the sail area into smaller individual sails makes them lighter and easier to handle.

Arguments against include: greater cost, more windage and weight aloft, less efficiency to windward, and more pieces of string to pull. To directly counter the 'small is beautiful' approach to sail plan design, I would add that to handle even the largest sail on a small or mid-size yacht is hardly going to tax the strength of most able-bodied sailors.

Ketches, yawls, and schooners, are often chosen for romantic reasons. There's nothing wrong with that, so long as it's understood. But if efficiency and economy is of more importance than a jaunty appearance, the sloop or cutter should be preferred.

Multihulls
Here I must express a personal interest. As well as designing and building them, I have sailed many different cats and tris during the last twenty years, and — with some notably ghastly exceptions — I have generally been impressed.

The *bete noir* of multihulls is capsize. But, as stability increases with size by the power of four (if of similar proportions, a 50' (15.24m) multi would be *sixteen* times more stable than one of 25' (7.62m)), the larger the boat, the less the risk.

Poor windward performance is another charge often levelled by those that know no better. This was perhaps true of earlier designs which, with their high windage and meagre leeway resistance, would emulate the proverbial barn when beating, but development has moved on apace.

A more valid criticism is the difficulty in parking the darned things. Many enthusiastic multihull sailors (myself included) have shed a hull or two in favour of a keelboat simply to enjoy the convenience of a marina. Of course, multihulls *are* welcomed in most marinas but, with a premium on width, their rates are likely to be awesome.

Construction

Without doubt, a crucial factor in selecting a boat is the material with which it is built. In a later section we'll go into the various horrors that can afflict the various materials so, for the while, let's summarise in general terms the respective trade-offs between virtues and vices.

GRP: An excellent boatbuilding material, loved by owners and manufacturers alike. Quite clearly the favourite of the vast majority of yachtsmen.

Despite the ogre of osmosis, GRP is both durable and relatively easy to maintain. The selection of yachts is enormous.

Wood — traditional: These techniques have remained virtually unchanged for centuries. Wooden boats undoubtedly require a more assiduous approach to maintenance, but they can be extremely long-lived if looked after.

Because such boats are an assemblage of thousands of separate pieces, bits can be whipped out and replaced as they deteriorate. Take *HMS Victory* for an example, launched in 1765 and virtually under continuous reconstruction ever since. As every year rolls by, less and less of her timbers are original, though, in every important regard, she remains much the same as the day she slid down the slipway.

Although a few boatyards still build yachts in the traditional way, the obvious expense of such craftsmanship severely limits their number. And with supply all but cut off, demand will certainly increase. The bedraggled, much-used old wooden boat of today, could be the valuable classic yacht of tomorrow — if properly restored and maintained.

Wood — modern techniques: Sophisticated glues have transformed wooden boatbuilding. Using a variety of laminating procedures — cold-moulding, strip planking, or a combination of these — such wooden hulls can be thought of as totally integrated, monocoque structures. Immensely strong, leak proof, and almost totally rot-resistant if properly treated, these methods have encouraged something of a renaissance for man's oldest boatbuilding material.

But, as with traditional methods, this is a labour intensive and costly process — usually reserved for racing or other specialised yachts. However, second-hand examples do come on to the market, and sometimes at reasonable prices.

And durability? Who knows — many have yet to wear out. I designed a few myself in the late sixties (when glues were relatively inferior) and, so far as I know, all that escaped accidents are still afloat. My money would be on the modern timber yacht proving to be a very tenacious stayer.

Steel: Often the long-distance sailor's first choice. Nothing absorbs punishment like steel. I've seen plating battered inwards more than a foot out of fair without puncturing.

Another advantage is ease of repair. No matter where you are, there will always be someone around with a welding torch and the skill to use it.

On the debit side, steel abominates neglect. Owners must wage an unremitting war on rust — with paint and a brush the most effective weapons. If corrosion really gets hold, then the decline can be rapid and irreversible.

Aluminium alloy: Similar to steel in many respects, but obviously much lighter.

At first thought aluminium would seem like the ideal material for boatbuilding — strong, corrosion resistant, and only a third the weight of steel. But few things are without their warts, and aluminium is no exception.

Most aluminium alloys are of a work-hardening type — a self-explanatory description which means they get harder and more brittle as they are bent or formed. This means that they can't

Steel plating can absorb an immense amount of punishment without breaching. Driven ashore onto rocks, this 26 footer was floated off on the next tide.

be hammered around with quite the same abandon as steel. Welding is also more difficult — calling for more elaborate (and expensive) equipment, and a meticulous approach to methods.

Galvanic corrosion can be a problem when aluminium is in contact with nobler metals and immersed in an electrolyte (seawater). Even copper or mercury based paints or antifoulings can lead to rapid degradation. Stray electrical currents leaking to earth can also do untold damage.

But perhaps one of the most infuriating characteristics of aluminium is that virtually nothing likes sticking to it — including paint. Often the ever-pragmatic French don't even bother to try. Their dull grey yachts are not a pretty sight.

Ferro-cement: More accurately 'ferro-concrete'. This undeniably unlovely material has had a bad press over the years — in many ways quite undeserved. Reviled by purist yacht owners, insurance, companies, and finance houses, amongst others, the 'rocker' has become the brutish outcast of the sailing world.

31

Personally, I don't entirely go along with this. Although there are certainly some awful examples about — invariably home built by people with more enthusiasm than skill — there are also some very fine yachts to be found.

Clearly no rocker is going to be a lightweight flyer, but if you are looking for something which, at a pinch, you could charter out as an ice-breaker, then it's worth a second thought.

When buying second-hand you can get a lot of ferro-cement boat for your money. Naturally, you must be careful in your choice — the good and the bad aren't always obviously distinguishable — but, given a modicum of caution, you could find just the boat you want at a very keen price indeed.

6 Seeing

When in pursuit of a boat the trail can be long and hard. And after some weeks following it, you can be sure any person will be almost delirious with relief when he turns that final corner and confronts the glorious object of his desire. Such moments don't lend themselves to restraint and wisdom. That first flash of recognition could be both irrational and unreasoned.

All this is perfectly understandable. No mere mortal can be expected to assess what he sees when his heart is singing like a thrush and his lips are stretched in a madman's grin. And yet, unless he comes to earth quickly, his wallet could find itself in the most deadly peril. This is boatings equivalent of the virgin's choice.

In the course of my business I am frequently amazed at some of the boats I'm instructed to examine. 'Could this really be the one?' I ask myself, staring with disbelief at the name peeling off the transom. Surely there must be some mistake — my client had seemed such a sensible fellow.

A catamaran I once looked over was so rotten my foot literally plunged through the plywood foredeck, doing no end of damage to my trousers. On another occasion a budding boat owner, seriously infected with the urge to get afloat, commissioned me to survey four different boats in as many weeks — the first three of which were in such awful condition I was astonished he had even given them a second thought. My combined fees for this last work — despite a compassionate 'quantity' discount to ease his pain — would have bought at least a couple of sails for the neat little craft he eventually found.

So, having located your boat and signalled your tentative interest to the owner or broker, it obviously befits you to appraise it sensibly before you even think of signing a sales agreement or parting with any cash. Your inspection will be no substitute for a professional survey (more on this in a later section), but it should help sift the geese from the swans before you get too involved in any ill-fated dealings.

And, remember, this is only a *provisional* inspection to see if it's worth proceeding further with the negotiations. Without the owner's express and prior permission, you aren't entitled to dismantle anything, poke around with spikes (except perhaps very lightly), or even scrape away antifouling to see what lies beneath. You will be limited to what you can see on the surface or within accessible spaces and lockers. Before a surveyor is let loose on a boat, a deposit will usually have been paid by the prospective buyer to cover any restitution costs which may arise from the survey. Within reason, the professional surveyor can delve as deeply as he considers necessary. But your position at this stage is still only that of a mildly interested viewer, with no agreements binding upon either party. It's therefore quite fair for the owner to expect you not to attack his property and to pay for any damage you might cause.

Having said that, some of the defects discussed below would probably only be discovered by using some mildly invasive investigation. For this you will require the nod from the owner. Don't be afraid to ask — through the broker, if there's one involved — specifying exactly what you would like to do. So long as you're not unreasonable, and can persuade him that he stands a fair chance of selling the boat to you if all goes well, most owners will agree.

The pre-purchase inspection kit

Simple equipment will help you make the most of your inspection. Toss the following items into a briefcase or bag and take them with you whenever you go to look at a boat:

a) *A camera.* The smaller and more compact the better. Personally, I find the capsule type ideal for the job. The one I use has automatic exposure and focus, and an in-built flash which triggers itself when the light level is too low. The focal

The basic inspection kit.

length of the lens is 35 mm, giving fairly wide-angle shots with a good depth of field. Mine is also weather-proof so I needn't treat it too daintily when it's raining.

Blaze away unstintingly — the inside, the outside, the underside, the lot. Even if you use a bagfull of films on a single boat, the cost will be insignificant compared to that of the whole.

Pay special attention to the more cluttered areas such as the foredeck and cockpit. Often it's not possible to absorb all the visual information at a single visit. Shots from different angles will provide you with the chance to review the various features later. If the details are still unclear, you can always have the relevant photos enlarged.

Photographs are especially valuable when you are considering more than one boat at a time. I look at boats on a daily basis, and confess to getting very confused sometimes. A boat surveyed on Monday may be distant history by Friday — unless I can nudge my brain cells with notes or other *aides memoir*.

b) *Notebook and pencil.* For jotting down both the obvious and less obvious points. Record your impressions as well as other details. If the colour of the berth cushions revolts you, make a note of it along with the cracked toilet bowl and the sagging hinge on a locker door.

c) *A torch*. Not the kind of massive device you could transfix enemy bombers with, but a small one which can be handily waved around inside small spaces. I find the *Maglite* type perfect for the purpose; the variable beam from broad flood to pin-point light is wonderful for illuminating the darker corners.

d) *A small articulated mirror*. A somewhat larger version of the ones dentists clatter against your teeth. These can be obtained from motor accessory shops at pretty low cost and are useful for peering into spaces too inaccessible to be seen by other means. Not absolutely necessary for a GRP boat, but invaluable on timber or steel where pockets of rot or rust may lurk in hidden corners.

e) *A pocket knife*. For the occasional illicit prod at suspicious looking timber. Remember your obligations to the owner, though.

Moisture Meters

No words on surveying impedimenta would be complete without reference to this modern equivalent of the divining rod. Since they became generally available in the late seventies, they have become both a boon and a curse to everyone involved in boat maintenance and repair.

They work by transmitting a low frequency radio field into the material under test and, by assessing changes in electrical capacitance, thereby detect the presence of moisture under the surface. As the moisture content varies, so does this electrical capacitance. These changes are displayed on a calibrated scale.

When backed up by other indications, this information is of value to the surveyor, but can be extremely misleading to the non-expert. I believe part of the confusion is caused by the way in which the so-called 'moisture content' is presented. Most meters give readings expressed as *percentages*, as if these figures actually represented the proportion of water contained in the laminate. Following a survey I am often asked what 'percentage' of water my moisture meter showed. If I was to answer truthfully, say, 'twenty two', my client might be forgiven for collapsing in a dead faint at my feet. The notion of nearly a quarter of one's hull being made up of water is enough to perturb the staunchest soul. 'My God, if it were a sponge I could wring it out!' I heard one man say.

Surveyors assess the moisture content of a hull by comparing readings taken on the underwater areas with those taken at corresponding stations on the topsides. As the topsides laminate can be considered to be more or less dry (except in certain circumstances) the difference between the two gives some indication of water absorption.

But readings may vary from day to day. Gelcoat — especially very *weathered* gelcoat — is quite porous and will retain surface moisture, perhaps after rain or a heavy dew. Damp hull linings *inside* the boat can also affect the readings. Salt deposits left by evaporated bilge water are hydroscopic and, again, can mislead the measurer. Recently, on a boat shortly to be the subject of litigation, I met the surveyor representing the other side. Using identical instruments, we worked our way around the hull. Not once did our readings agree.

So, be warned. If you hear a man quoting absolute figures, treat him with vast suspicion. You can be pretty sure he speaketh as from the east end of a westbound bull.

I shall cover this more fully in the section on *osmosis* but, in the meantime, it's sufficient to appreciate that moisture meters are not for casual use. They are a undoubtedly a useful tool for the professional, but the information they give should be interpreted in conjunction with other factors. Anyway, in the final event there's probably nothing to beat an experienced eye.

And bear in mind that the purpose of any inspection is not to *condemn* (people often ask me if boat has 'passed' its survey) but to see a boat exactly for what it is. The most important thing is to *know*. Most defects are repairable so, provided you buy at the right price and are prepared to do the work, even quite a run down yacht could still be an attractive purchase.

What follows is a guide to some of the most common defects you should watch out for, and how best to find them. I have started with problems uniquely associated with timber, then GRP, then steel. The last part covers general areas which would be common to all.

The paragraphs in italics describe briefly what may be required to rectify these defects. It's beyond the scope of this book to go into too much detail but, hopefully, the descriptions will give you some idea of the nature of the remedial work and, by implication, the likely magnitude of cost involved.

7 Timber

Without wishing to dwell too long on very elementary matters, a brief description of constructional methods might be helpful. These are:-

Carvel planked: Here the planks are laid edge to edge. The seams between them are then caulked with cotton or oakum, and 'payed' (filled), usually with red lead putty beneath the waterline, and white lead putty above. A variant is *splined carvel* where thin strips of wood are glued into the seams — often for decorative purposes on varnished topsides where putty would be unsightly.

Strip planked: Similar to carvel but the planks are usually much narrower and the edges are glued together. Sometimes the edges of the planks are profiled (Fig. 1, p.41) for ease of fitting and to increase the 'faying' area of the glue line.

Clinker planked: Also 'clencher' and 'lapstrake' (in the U.S.). The overlapping planking favoured by ancient Norsemen and surviving on smaller boats to this day. With the exception of some bastardised methods using glued overlapping strakes (often of plywood), clinker planking is never caulked. It relies for its watertightness on the precision with which the 'lands' (overlaps) are made.

Cold moulded: Cold moulded hulls are made by laminating thin strips of timber *in situ*. Often these are applied diagonally, first one way then the other, with the outside laminate being laid fore-and-aft to simulate carvel planking.

Sheet plywood: This cheap and cheerful form of construction was very popular during the fifties and sixties, but has since been virtually abandoned for more sophisticated techniques. Easily recognisable by the characteristic chined hull sections.

Outside

The eye of the beholder: Very often, the first sight of a wooden boat is the most telling. Stand back and take in the overview.

If she is blocked off ashore look for 'hogging' — the downward droop of bow and stern, as if she had been jacked up in the middle — and 'sagging', which is the opposite. Take a squint from ahead and astern to see is she is 'wrung' (twisted). If any of these conditions are very pronounced, then that's pretty bad news; the structure has been seriously strained and the fastenings and joints are so loose that the hull will literally flop into just about any position she's left in. And, even if that's not the case and in truth she's as tight as a drum, the only other possible cause would be such lamentable workmanship as would certainly turn you off her.

The ear of the beholder: Timber hulls will tell you quite a lot about themselves if you're prepared to listen. Amongst other things, tapping along the planking can reveal rot, the presence of marine borers, and delamination in cold moulded or plywood construction. For this purpose, surveyors usually use a light rawhide or plastic headed hammer, but even a knuckle will do non-destructive (at least to the boat) service.

Healthy planking will sound firm and resonant when struck; rotten and wormy areas will sound dead — even soft; delamination will sound hollow, and may 'click' as the separated layers slap against each other.

But don't be fooled by changes in tone due to the internal structure. Whack the outside of the hull on a large sawn frame or floor and it will sound quite different to unsupported planking. External suspicion should prompt further internal inspection.

Hard chines where they shouldn't ought to be: Obviously the sections of a round bilged hull should be smooth and fair. If you see a pronounced knuckle anywhere then there's a fair chance that there are some broken frames lurking inside.

Seams — the open and shut case: It's a well know fact that wood shrinks and swells with variations in its moisture content. Typically, hull planking will 'open up' when the boat is ashore in dry conditions (the topsides can do this even when afloat —

First impressions are important. Take in the overview before getting down to the details.

Hard angles or knuckles on the outside of a carvel hull often mean cracked timbers within.

especially in the summer) and will slowly 'plim up' again after the vessel is relaunched. This second process may take a few days, and will probably necessitate some energetic pumping until the leakage staunches itself.

If a boat has been ashore for some years, the seams can be very wide indeed. In this case it is also likely that the caulking will have loosened, dried, and become useless.

Excessive shrinkage can loosen the fastenings. Timber shrinks much more across the grain than it does along the grain's axis. This promotes a differential movement between the planks and frames (Fig. 2, p.41) which introduces a powerful shearing action on the rivets.

How this should all be dealt with is very much a matter of judgement. If the seams are unacceptably wide, and the caulking in poor condition, then they will require raking out and recaulking. Recaulking just part of a seam is rarely effective. As you tamp the cotton into one place, the rest of the seam widens, and, before you know it, you find yourself doing the whole length.

If, however, the seams have simply opened up to a 'normal' extent then the boat can be re-launched and, in due course, all will be well. The advice of a surveyor or experienced shipwright should be sought.

Split seams — strip planking: A more serious defect than on a conventionally planked carvel hull, as the integrity of the glue lines is crucial to watertightness.

Resist the temptation to fill the seam with more glue or any other hard filler. For when the planking plims up it will simply jack itself further apart on this unyielding material, and the split will extend still further. The best solution is to open up the seam with a router and straight cutter (using a batten pinned to the hull as a guide) and to glue in a spline. Routers can be as uncontrollable as supermarket trolleys so, unless you're a dab hand with such tools, this is definitely a job best left to the professional.

Prominent fillers and corroded fastenings: Inspect the topsides and underwater areas for raised filler pellets — which may be either wooden 'grain pins' (often incorrectly called dowels) or hardened synthetic stoppers. Some may already have

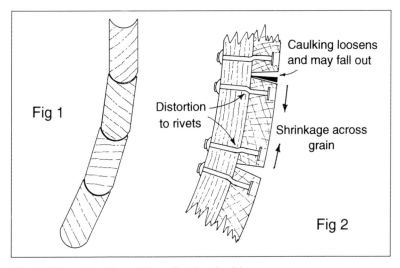

Fig. 1: 'Thumbnail' profiling of strip planking.
Fig. 2: Rivets pulled out of shape by shrinkage of planking.

fallen out or may be loose enough to be removed with a finger nail.

Although the cause may be quite innocent, the filler could have been burst outwards by corrosion to the fastening beneath (Fig. 3). If the head of the fastening is exposed, examine it closely. Give it a bit of a scratch to see is the metal is bright beneath the surface.

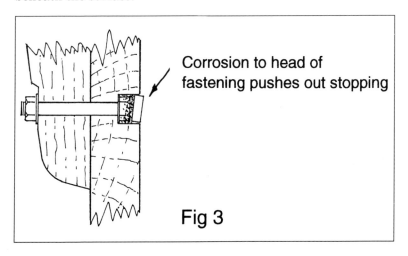

Surveyors will usually draw sample hood end fastenings (which secure the ends of each plank at bow and stern) to check for corrosion. This is beyond the scope of your less stringent inspection, but you may get a hint of what lies beneath by looking at the state of the filler.

Refastening a riveted boat is always a time consuming and costly business. Each defective rivet has to be removed, and another rivet (of larger diameter, otherwise it would be loose in the hole) inserted and peened over. Of course, all the original work was done with the hull conveniently empty. Subsequent repairs will be far more awkward.

Rust weeps: Another symptom of corrosion — this time to iron or steel fastenings. The planking of cheap and heavy forms of construction — typically, converted work boats — is often fastened with iron (or, worse still, galvanised steel) cut nails known as 'dumps'. If a significant proportion of these are badly corroded then the hull will require complete refastening.

But if, for the most part, the hull is copper fastened, then the odd rusty ferrous fastening may not be too serious. Iron bolts are often used to secure knees, transverse floors, engine beds, chain plates, and other meaty structural components.

Corroded dumps are very difficult to remove. It is usually better just to leave them in place, and drive in new fastenings between them. Severely corroded ferrous bolts must be taken out and replaced. As with the rivets, this can either be a simple or difficult task, depending upon internal access.

Electrochemical softening: Stray electrical currents can cause a timber's natural acidity to turn alkaline, resulting in localised softening. Most woods are intolerant of alkalis. They eat away at the cellulose and lignin that binds the fibres together and causes them to separate. Indeed, this very process is used in the breaking down of wood pulp for paper production.

Mahogany planked hulls are particularly susceptible. Take a discreet prod around any earthing plates, sacrificial anodes, and any metal skin fittings that may be sites of electrical activity (possibly galvanic). If any of these fittings appear to have been drawn unnaturally into the timber, this is always cause for suspicion, certainly warranting inspection by an expert.

Affected areas should be cut away and replaced. Personally, I believe it helps to re-locate earthing plates and anodes — the major offenders — on a periodic basis to prevent the onset of this problem.

Before we take a look at the interior, a word or two on timber's natural enemy wouldn't go amiss.

The ravages of rot: Coniophora Puteana and *Serpula Lachrymans* are two characters you certainly wouldn't want to see on your crew list. These fungal stowaways are better known as wet rot and dry rot. The first is by far the most common, the second the most pernicious.

Wooden hulls rarely rot on the outside — or, if they do, it probably started on the inside and worked its way through. In fact, salt water is a fairly effective fungicide, actually inhibiting fungal decay. Poorly ventilated, dark, damp corners are what these microscopic monsters relish — and there are plenty of those inside the typical wooden yacht.

With wet rot there is some darkening of the wood (obviously impossible to see if painted) and it may crack longitudinally along the grain. Often there is a shell of sound timber over a rotten core; you will see this frequently in deck beams, where the decay creeps in from the ends, leaving them looking deceptively healthy from the outside.

Dry rot is distinguishable by shrinkage of the wood and cracking *across* the grain. Again the wood darkens — appearing almost charred in some cases. And the wood becomes much lighter in weight — quite discernible if you crumble a bit away in your fingers. Dry rot also has a distinctive musty smell — often the first indication when you board a boat for the first time.

Rotten planking can sometimes be seen externally as slightly sunken areas, often covered with lifting, crinkled paint. But it will be inside where you will uncover the most spectacular horrors. Remember; airless, dark and damp. Use your hands to feel up under the sidedecks and into other corners you can't see. Inspect joints where water can enter and lie. Look for darkened patches of varnish — again usually around joints. Truly rotten wood will yield even to finger pressure, but it may need some poking around with a spike to reveal less advanced decay.

And, if you find that rot has really got a grip, then it's a fair bet that there's more you haven't found. If the phrase 'rotten as a carrot' seems somewhat hard on the carrot, then this is obviously a boat to walk away from.

Although many 'instant' cures have come and gone, there is no real alternative other than to cut away and replace all infected areas. To buy a rotten boat and attempt piece-meal restoration is to get some idea how Sisyphus felt — condemned to roll a huge boulder ceaselessly up a hill, never to reach the top.

Inside

Down below: Take a good sniff when you reach the bottom of the companionway. Fresh and sharp, like a pine grove in springtime — or more reminiscent of the bottom of a laundry basket? Foul smell, foul boat, one old shipwright I knew would say — and there's a lot of truth in that.

Cracked frames: The plimming up of planking can exert fearsome tensions on the frames (ribs) of a boat. This can be a particular problem if hard fillers such as white lead putty or knifing stopper have been used (instead of the softer red lead putty) to pay the seams beneath the waterline.

Light, steamed timbers are the most susceptible, but even heavy sawn or grown frames aren't immune. Look where the bend is tightest — garboards and turn of the bilge — and alongside the rivets where the timber is weakened by the hole (Fig. 4).

Sawn frames can crack, either through structural damage or shrinkage, if the grain diverges too far from the line of the frame itself (Fig. 5).

On older boats you will very often find cracked frames which have already been doubled up to strengthen them. If you find many more on one side than the other, suspect some accident in its history.

Replacing frames is usually impracticable and unnecessary. But a serviceable repair can achieved by adding a 'doubler' just forward or aft of the cracked frame. Such doublers should, where possible, extend at least two full plank widths each side of the crack.

Sawn frames can be repaired by strapping over the crack, either with wood or metal.

If possible lift the cabin sole to see what lurks beneath.

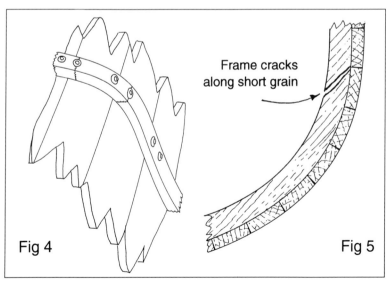

Fig. 4: Look for cracked ribs where the curves are tightest.
Fig. 5: Sawn frames crack where the grain is shortest.

Interior metalwork: Many wooden boats utilised iron or steel (and sometimes, if you're lucky, bronze) structural components in the hull and deck. These can include frames, transverse floors, strap floors, hanging or lodging knees, breasthooks, deck beams, and of course the fastenings. Sometimes the internal framings are predominantly of metal — known as 'composite construction' — and sometimes metal has just been used to beef up certain areas.

Either way, rust is the obvious demon you should be wary of. The replacement of buried bits and pieces can be astonishingly expensive.

On Deck

The first thing to establish is how the deck is made. This may seem like daft advice, but it isn't always apparent. The planking could be, teak, iroko, pitch pine, or sometimes Douglas fir, and can be either solid or laid over a plywood base for decorative effect. Sheet plywood decks are also fairly common. Coverings could be canvas, GRP, or one of the proprietary systems — Cascover, Trakmark, et cetera. Once you know what you've got, you can look at it sensibly.

Plywood: Here you will find your feet amazingly good diviners of trouble. Feel for soft spots which may be rot or delamination. Tap around a bit to confirm your suspicions. Look especially at butted and exposed panel edges where the end grain could have absorbed water.

Small areas can be locally repaired, but rot or delamination in one spot augers badly for the rest. Actually, re-decking in plywood is sometimes less costly than it seems. Large panels go on quickly.

Teak on ply: Decorative and waterproof — the two prime claims of this technique. And, so long as the workmanship is good and the caulking in sound condition, also tolerably durable.

Examine the payed seams closely. If whatever compound has been used (polyurethane, polysulphide, but hardly ever bitumen) is breaking down, it will certainly be allowing water to penetrate.

Feel for any pronounced spring or buckling in the teak cladding — a sure sign of separation between the two layers.

Also look for 'cupping' (Fig. 6) of the surface across the grain of individual planks; again the bond must have failed.

Voids beneath the teak are obviously worrying. Damp, dark, and warmed by sunshine — could any self-respecting rot spore ask for more?

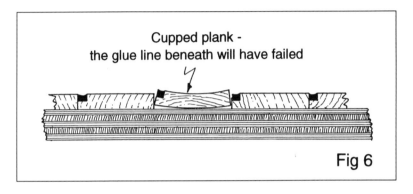

Cupped plank -
the glue line beneath will have failed

Fig 6

Solid planking: Usually known as a 'laid' deck. The 'V' section seams are usually caulked with cotton, and then either payed with synthetic compounds or a vile bituminous concoction known as 'marine glue'.

And as with hulls, so with decks. The planks shrink and plim in exactly the same manner — responding alternately to sunshine and rain. Softwoods — pitch pine and Douglas fir — are especially prone. Teak moves much less but, because it is such an oily wood, it is often difficult to get mastics or glue to stick to it.

Getting a bit thin on top?: Feet, scrubbing brushes, and the occasional application of sandpaper will all play their part in gradually scouring away the planking.

If very worn, the signs of this will be observable up on deck. Get down on your hands and knees and look at where the planking adjoins the cabin sides or any permanent deck fitting. The original level of the upper surface of the deck should easily be seen (Fig. 7, p.48).

Another indicator is the state of the grain pins. Some may be worn away entirely, exposing the screw-head beneath; others could have fallen out, in which case the wear to what was once a deeply counter-bored hole will be immediately evident.

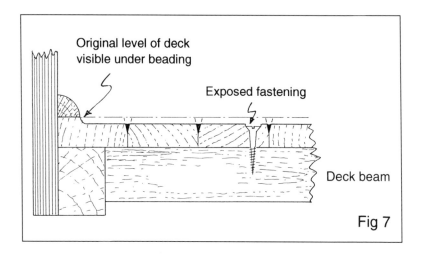

Fig 7

The seamy side of sailing: With wear, the square rebated seams commonly used on teak clad decks will eventually become too shallow to effectively hold the caulking (an ordinary pin, pushed down through the paying, is a useful implement for determining this). And the 'V' seams used on laid decks obviously get progressively narrower the lower you go. As the general condition and integrity of the seams is the main defence against leaking, you will certainly want to pay particular attention to them.

Leaking synthetic filled seams should be raked out and re-payed. It's usually pointless just to smear in more mastic. The inevitable accumulations of dirt in the crevices will prevent proper adhesion.

Cracked marine glue can be temporarily rejuvenated by running a heated iron along the seam to re-melt the bead. However, there is a limit to how often you can do this before you must face the inevitable and start again.

A walk in the wet stuff: In some respects, rainy days are to be preferred when looking at wooden boats. Of course we all like to stroll around in the sunshine, but you will learn much more about the condition of the decks when it's bucketing down.

Below in the cabin, the gruesome effects of any leaks will be only too apparent. And, as you walk over teak-on-ply decks, a footstep in one place might produce a little squirt of water in another — vividly demonstrating a problem which might otherwise have gone unnoticed.

8 Glass Reinforced Plastic (GRP)_____

Topsides

Let's face it, if we wanted to take good care of our boats we wouldn't put them anywhere near the water. A few seasons' service afloat will soon strip that showroom lustre from any yacht. Docking in your marina berth, rafting up with friends, even coming alongside in a dinghy — all are potentially damaging manoeuvres which are bound to leave scars, no matter how careful you might be.

Also, of course, the weather will take its toll. The combination of sunlight and salt water will gnaw inexorably at the gelcoat. Gradually it will degrade; eventually, after very many years, it will be destroyed altogether.

Fading: The first visible results of this weathering process. The gelcoat takes on a chalky appearance with variations in colour density. On dark-coloured hulls, this is very easy to see, but you will have to look more closely on white.

If the condition isn't too advanced, the appearance of topside gelcoat can be improved by polishing with wax polishes. Those containing silicones — most car types — should be avoided as they can contaminate the surface and make future painting or repair more difficult. More severe fading will require cutting back with a mild abrasive paste — such as T-Cut or Farecla — before polishing. Although this can be done by hand, an electric rotary polisher with a foam pad will do wonders in a fraction of the time.

Abrasions: Minor physical damage will show itself in the inevitable collection of scuffs and scratches the topsides will attract. Although obviously a matter of degree, for the most part such damage is only cosmetically significant. The most vulnerable areas are at midlength (where the hull is fattest), at the turn of the transom, and around the bow where the anchor can do its awful worst. Often you will find inexpert repairs —

more unsightly than the original damage, but at least giving some protection.

The most minor abrasions can often be removed by lightly abrading the surface with fine wet-or-dry abrasive paper (400 grit, then 1000 grit used wet), and finally restoring the shine with an abrasive paste. Deeper scratches — and certainly those that go right through to the laminate — should first be filled with catalysed matching gelcoat (thickened slightly with colloidal silica), before fairing and polishing as above. To make an invisible repair takes some skill and is best entrusted to an expert if you are in any way uncertain of your own abilities. As I've mentioned already, a badly executed repair can look worse than the original defect.

Gelcoat crazing: These appear as hairline cracks in the gelcoat, and are either caused by impact damage or excessive flexure of the laminate. Minor localised impact damage — often known as *star crazing* because it radiates from a central point — is usually a relatively minor defect, of very little structural significance.

More extensive crazing could be less trivial. The vessel could have been involved in a fairly serious collision, or been crushed (say, between a quay and a much heavier boat), or may have dropped off a large wave to crash sideways into the trough. Whatever the cause, there is probably some associated damage to the interior structure which you should look for.

Although called gelcoat crazing, it's likely that the damage actually extends deeper into the laminate itself, and there may even be some delamination of the layers of GRP which you cannot see. Simply filling the surface cracks would be a pointless exercise — it would achieve nothing structurally and the cracks will almost certainly reappear when the panel flexes in service. The affected areas should be ground right back to sound laminate (deeper than the cracks or delamination), and the GRP made good in proper fashion. Finally, of course, the gelcoat must be restored by filling, fairing, and polishing.

Thinning gelcoat: Pinholes are a sure sign that the gelcoat is nearing the end of its useful life. The endless cycle of weathering and polishing gradually erodes it away until the tiny air bubbles it contains are exposed (Fig. 8). A few isolated

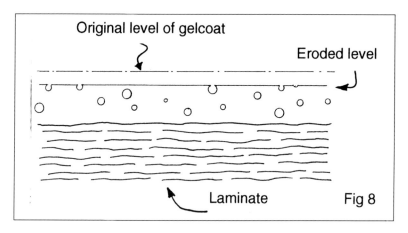

Fig 8

pinholes are no great cause for concern, but if the gelcoat is extensively peppered then early action may be advisable.

On paler gelcoats which have thinned, the darker laminate beneath can often be seen 'shadowing' through. This is best seen in bright sunlight, standing back a few feet so you can view a largish area at a time.

Painting the topsides is the only solution — preferably with a two-part or moisture-cured polyurethane. But it's not enough to simply apply a gloss paint directly over a pinholed surface. The surface tension of the paint film will draw it away from the lip of the hole and you will end up with a deeper and more conspicuous pinhole than you started out with! After priming the surface, the pinholes should first be filled before overpainting — a tedious and time-consuming process which all adds to the cost.

Although I have seen some excellent paint jobs successfully applied by skilled (or lucky) amateurs, the potential for cock-ups can be many and spectacular. Practise on a small area first.

All that glisters is not gelcoat: There is a product known as *Owatrol*™ which will impart an almost miraculous shine to weathered and faded gelcoat. Simply wipe it on with a soft cloth and, within minutes, you can stand back and admire your reflection in the resultant gloss. However, these results are far from permanent (the manufacturers make no claims that they are) and the treatment needs repeating on a more or less annual basis.

For the prospective purchaser there is an obvious trap.

Always be wary of the older boat which shines like new. The gleaming hull you admire so much may not be in such immaculate condition as you think — and could look as ragged as an old barn door in a few months time.

Of course, it may have been painted, but you can easily tell the difference. *Owatrol* is identifiable by its transparency. On darker hulls, fading can usually be seen beneath the shine, showing up as inconsistencies in colour density. And look out for slight swirl marks where it has been wiped on — quite dissimilar from the orange-peel effect of a sprayed finish or the obvious marks of the paintbrush.

None of this is intended to knock *Owatrol* itself, which will breathe temporary new life into an old gelcoat quite splendidly. But if it's used to deceive, then the buyer should beware. It's important to see a boat for what it is — perhaps just a tired old girl recently tarted up for sale.

Hull — underwater areas

Osmosis: The dreaded 'O' word, the ring of which will make grown men swoon. Otherwise known as 'boat pox' — a charmless but apt description.

Most substances are absorbent to some extent, and polyester resin is no exception. Hailed in the early days as the 'everlasting material' it proved to have its susceptibilities as any other.

The word 'osmosis' actually describes a process rather than a condition. It is, more correctly, the mechanism by which a fluid of lesser viscosity will pass through a semi-permeable membrane to dilute a higher viscosity fluid on the other side. But it has been adopted by the boating world as a generic term covering all forms of water absorption — or, more precisely, all *discernible* forms of water absorption. Really, to say a boat has osmosis is a bit like saying that your aunt has breathing — assuming she still has, of course.

But the classic liquid filled blisters found on some hulls *are* the result of the osmotic process. Described simply, it begins with water penetrating the gelcoat — which we should think of as micro-porous. Once in contact with the laminate itself, the water starts to dissolve both the binders used to hold the fibreglass (chopped strand mat) together, and other chemicals loose in the laminate. This 'soup' of various chemical substances

Hunting for blisters. Look from the shade towards the light.

is of greater viscosity than sea-water, which is now attracted osmotically through the gelcoat. Considerable pressures can be built up within the blisters — evidence of the power of this mechanism.

Prominent blisters can usually be spotted without removing the antifouling — though, of course, they would be far easier to see on a stripped hull. Crouch down low under the turn of the bilge, and look obliquely upwards towards the light. Any irregularity in the surface profile caused by larger blisters should be apparent. A non-destructive alternative to scraping off patches of antifouling is simply to douse it with water. Even quite small prominences will be visible on a wet and shiny surface.

And, if the antifouling is dry, look for signs of weeping from a burst blister. Take some of the fluid onto a finger-tip and give it a sniff; it will probably smell strongly of vinegar — the acetic acid from the dissolved binder. This smell is absolutely characteristic of osmotic blistering.

Wicking: The wicked younger brother of full-blown osmosis — also known as *fibre aligned blistering.*

53

This is an easily understood process. Again, water is absorbed through the gelcoat. Once there, it is then carried by capillary action along the glass fibres lying immediately beneath the gelcoat, causing them to swell slightly. As the condition becomes more advanced, small but distinct blisters form along the line of the affected fibres, patterning the gelcoat surface in lines of raised welts corresponding to the actual lay of the fibres.

Wicking is almost impossible to see with the antifouling in place. The prominences are small and usually obliterated by the thick paint. Even on a bare hull, it can be tricky to discern in its early stages. Some people (especially enraged owners disputing its presence) can't even see it when it's pointed out to them.

So, what is its significance? Although not as dramatic as osmotic blistering, all forms of water absorption are progressive in nature and should be discouraged. Wicking can (though doesn't always) develop into osmotic blistering. It's very common to find the two conditions together on the same hull.

But it's also important to put these defects into perspective. In my years as a yacht surveyor I have only seen a handful of boats so severely afflicted as to be dangerous. And, in each case, the osmosis was only a symptom of more serious problems — an under-cured or resin-starved laminate, for example. Most yachts with osmosis could soldier on for years — even if left untreated.

Perhaps the profoundest effect is upon the *value* of the vessel. For a whole osmosis industry has sprung up, eager to make profits from misfortune. Such is the paranoia and panic induced by this condition, that even a hint of it can wipe thousands of pounds off the selling price of an otherwise excellent boat.

Clearly, these considerations are of importance to the purchaser. Many people will shrink from buying at the very thought of a few small blisters. In my view this can be a mistake. In almost every case, rectification is both possible and effective. Buy at the right price, have the hull repaired, and you could come out way ahead of the game.

The treatment for both osmosis and wicking is the same. Notwithstanding anything you might hear at the yacht club bar, there are no short cuts — no way to sweeten the medicine. At the outset you should seek the advice of a surveyor — firstly, to confirm the diagnosis, and then to oversee the treatment.

Many surveyors advocate the entire removal of the gelcoat, but in my opinion, this is only rarely necessary. Aggressive abrasion of the gelcoat by grit-blasting will remove the antifouling, knock out any blisters or other 'soft spots', and leave a wonderful key for the protective coatings. Gelcoat peeling (by a machine like an electric planer) will also give good results but, as it removes a constant thickness from the surface (regardless of good or bad), it isn't as selective as blasting. Some peelers leave such a smooth finish that it's advisable to lightly blast the surface afterwards — an additional expense.

After hosing off to remove the dust and any chemical residues, the hull should be allowed to dry. Many professional repairers use infra-red heaters or dehumidifiers to accelerate this process, but satisfactory results can be obtained by waiting for the hull to dry naturally — perhaps over the duration of the winter lay-up — with the boat outside. In this case, it's advisable to tape a short plastic skirt from just above the waterline, so that rainwater can drip free.

*The final stage is to overcoat with successive coats of one of the proprietary solvent-free epoxy resins. These should be applied (usually with a foam roller) strictly in accordance with the manufacturer's instructions. The voids left by blisters and other flaws will be filled with a compatible filler, knifed on **top** of the first coat. And each coat of resin must be applied within a defined 'time window' to allow it to bond properly to the one beneath it — leave it too long and you will have to abrade the entire surface again to provide an adequate key.*

*The most important point to remember is that **time** is the great healer. To rush the job before the laminate has dried thoroughly is to seal the defects into the hull, ready to emerge at a later date. A very wet laminate could take several months in the open air to dry to satisfactorily levels. Preferable by far to lose half a season's sailing, than to have to repeat the whole grisly process in a couple of years time.*

If you plan to do the work yourself, you will need to allocate a continuous block of time (with good weather, if working outside) to actually slap on the resin. Five or six days should be set aside — though, actually, you will only require perhaps a couple of hours each day. With our capricious climate, this isn't always easy to plan in advance. For the working man, this can be a problem.

Also, resist the temptation to skimp on materials. Having paid for the grit-blasting and waited so long, it would be downright silly to fall into the ha'p'orth-of-tar trap. The very minimum of four coats of epoxy should be applied — five would be better. Unfortunately, certain manufacturers seek to make their products more attractive by claiming that you can get away with less. You can — but not for very long; so, if you want a durable job, ignore such claims. When talking about protective barriers, there is quite obviously a relationship between the thickness of a coating and the protection it will grant. The more coats the merrier, say I.

If the work is to be done professionally, then check into the exact specification before you commit yourself. And have a qualified surveyor monitor the drying process. Most boatyards are honestly run outfits, but there are some that might hurry a job along in order to get your cheque a little earlier. If obliged to wait for the thumb's up from your surveyor, there's not much they can do but be patient.

Stress crazing: A form of gelcoat crazing brought on by acute flexure of a laminate.

The sea is a lumpy old place and any hull must be expected to take a hammering in heavy going. Some flexing of the hull shell is both natural and desirable. Within reason it will do no damage, provided that the stresses are absorbed gradually into the yacht's structure as a whole. However, if this benign flexing is abruptly restricted by structural 'hard spots' then the material can fatigue and, in due course, fail.

Such hard spots are usually caused by the boat's internal structure — bulkheads, soles, bunk bases, et cetera. A common situation is illustrated in Figure 9. Here a thin plywood bulkhead is bonded directly to the inside surface of the hull shell. Forward and aft of the bulkhead, the hull flexes within its elastic limits, comfortably absorbing the buffeting of the waves. But that narrow, unyielding edge brings all movement to an abrupt halt, generating an immense concentration of stress along the line where the bulkhead abuts the hull.

Planing type power boats, with their low deadrise hulls, are especially prone to this form of damage. I have seen hulls

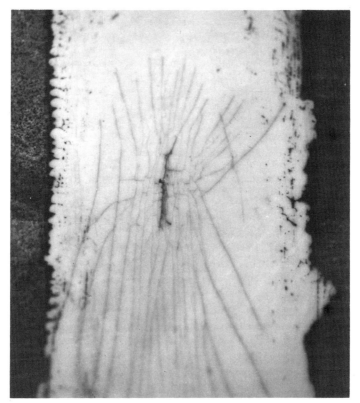

Typical stress crazing. When ground away for repair it was found that the dark crack in the centre had penetrated right through the laminate

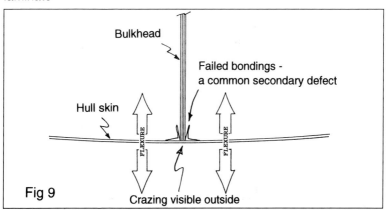

Bulkhead

Failed bondings -
a common secondary defect

Hull skin

FLEXURE

FLEXURE

Fig 9

Crazing visible outside

cracked right through along the line of a bulkhead, as neatly as if someone had taken a saw to it.

Stress crazing can usually be seen through the antifouling — indeed thick antifouling can make it more obvious. The forward sections of a boat take the most punishment, and this is the first place to look. In power boats, the areas under the engine bearers are also vulnerable. Tap along the outside of the hull listening for the dead sound of internal structural components. Then examine the surface carefully for cracks. If you find any, also look inside for associated damage — failed bulkhead bondings are a common secondary characteristic.

Quite apart from the structural implications, cracks below the waterline provide a ready path for water to enter the laminate. If there is delamination as well, or the boat has been afloat for a long time, then there could also be a lateral migration of moisture away from the point of entry.

If the stress crazing is limited to a fairly small area, then repair can be both easy and effective. But if much of the internal structure appears to be struggling to break through to the outside, then either the boat has suffered a serious accident

On planing hulls, examine the outboard faces of the spray rails. The sharp angles of the laminate are a potentially weak point.

Loose stock: Not a stampede of cows, but movement between the rudder blade and the stainless steel bar on which it turns. Fix the tiller or wheel (most easily by having someone hold it) and give the blade a rotational wiggle. Any movement will be discernible at the point where the stock emerges from the blade.

Very slight movement isn't usually of much consequence. The tangs have probably slightly enlarged the pockets in which they are embedded. But if the movement is very pronounced, then something must be done. Either one or more of the tangs has come away from the stock, or the filler within the blade has broken down completely.

In serious cases, repair would necessitate splitting the mouldings, examining and replacing the stock if broken, and then reassembling the whole caboodle. Personally, I believe that a better (and often cheaper) alternative would be to make a new rudder altogether — this time fitting a shaped plywood core to the stock, and glassing over for strength and durability.

Repairs can sometimes be effected by locating the tangs from outside (by using the kind of metal detector DIYers use when looking for pipes, etc.,), cutting in through the mouldings from both sides, and refilling the void so that the tang is firmly gripped.

Decks

If anything, GRP decks lead an even less enviable life than hulls. True, they are not continuously immersed in water, but all sorts of other abuses are literally heaped upon them.

In common with the topsides, they will collect their quota of knocks, scratches, and crazing. Guests will leap aboard with elephantine grace, or tramp with gritty shoes into the cockpit; butter-fingered crew members will drop spinnaker poles and anchors; and all the while those ideally receptive horizontal planes will be offered up to the bleaching effects of the ultra-violet light from above.

Luckily, of course, this is all very visible, and a gentle saunter around the decks will soon tell you what sort of shape they are in. General repairs will be much in line with those to the hull, with the exception that wax polishes should never be used — not unless you want to issue your crew with crampons, that is.

So, let's move on to defects specific to GRP decks:

Core separation: As you walk over the deck, listen for creaking noises beneath your feet — especially in areas where the surface 'springs' more than usual.

Creaking is caused by movement between components. It could simply be the deck flexing downwards to touch, say, a moulded inner liner or unbonded bulkhead, but, in the case of a GRP deck, it is more likely to be core separation. This is a very common defect, usually resulting from careless manufacture.

Decks are often stiffened by sandwiching panels of end-grain balsa within the laminate. To understand the problem, it helps to understand the manufacturing process. First, the gelcoat is applied to the mould and, once hardened, the layers of GRP which will form the outer laminate are then laid up. Whilst these layers are still soft and sticky, pre-shaped panels of end-grain balsa (made up of small squares of wood mounted on a glass scrim for flexibility) are pressed down onto the surface and rolled flat. Finally, the layers of GRP which form the inner skin are added, and the laminate is complete.

Now, because balsa wood is obviously opaque, it is difficult for the laminator to ensure that there are no voids beneath it when he lays it down on that wet fibreglass mat. Of course, it should be possible for him to work systematically over the balsa, carefully pressing every bit of it into place. But we live in an imperfect world, and GRP laminating is a pretty dreadful job which doesn't always attract the quality of labour it deserves. If the work is done sloppily, then voids between the outer laminate and the balsa core will be the inevitable result (Fig. 11).

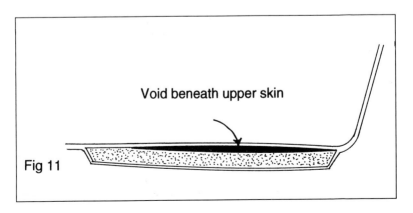

Void beneath upper skin

Fig 11

Its significance depends very much upon degree. If very small areas are found, they can be ignored, unless they are in way of deck fittings where water could enter to possibly cause rot (balsa is non-durable). But if the deck creaks its protest with nearly every step, then it may need to be repaired.

This will entail drilling numerous strategically placed small holes through the upper surface of the deck and injecting a medium viscosity, solvent-free epoxy resin into the voids with a syringe. The deck should be weighted down while this cures and, afterwards, the holes themselves will have to be repaired — usually simply by filling with matching gelcoat.

Although DIY is possible, this is an awkward and messy job, perhaps better left to a professional boat repairer.

That spring in your step: The sensation that you are walking across a trampoline can be extremely disconcerting. This defect is usually found on smaller, lightly-built boats, where the builders have pared down the scantlings to less than is sensible. Such flexibility might be acceptable on a hatch box or doghouse top, where you won't need to stand too often, but would be more worrying on side or foredecks.

Although unlikely to fail completely — except in extreme circumstances — a springy deck is evidence of poor design or over-light construction. Don't expect such a boat to be long lived.

Decks can be stiffened by adding beams or glassing stringers to the underside, but this is rarely worth it on the type of boat on which it occurs.

Teak on GRP: A nicely laid teak deck can do a lot to soften the clinical aspects of all that fibreglass, and is a frequent and well regarded 'extra' on better quality boats. Thin strips of teak are bedded to the deck — either with epoxy or the same mastic used to pay the seams — and are fastened with stainless steel self tapping screws, run through the upper surface of the GRP into the balsa core. Figure 12 (p.64) shows a typical section.

Apart from general wear, teak decks are fairly trouble free, but one particular problem has far reaching implications of which you should be wary. If the bonding between the timber and GRP is imperfect, and the integrity of the seams breaks down, then water can seep all the way through to the balsa core.

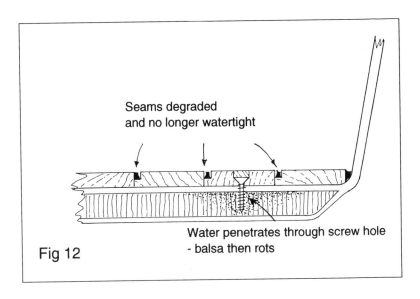

Seams degraded
and no longer watertight

Fig 12

Water penetrates through screw hole
- balsa then rots

Lovely to look at, but what problems may lie beneath?

Balsa, as a matter of interest, is technically a hardwood — despite its light weight and soft texture. But it's also non-durable and will rot away with gusto, especially if contained in damp, sun-warmed panels such as decks.

There isn't much you can do to determine the condition of the balsa from above, but sponginess in the core can sometimes be felt underneath by pressing upwards on the thin GRP covering which forms the lower 'slice' of the sandwich. Always be wary of teak on GRP decks if they are in obviously poor condition. The notion that they can be spruced up just by cleaning and repaying, can sometimes fall grossly short of the mark.

Hull/Deck Joint

Some years ago, after a severe storm, the deck of a fair sized sailboat was found floating off Cape Hatteras in the United States. The hull — and the crew along with it — had disappeared. When examined closely, it was evident that the aluminium 'pop' type rivets holding the two mouldings together had simply come unzipped — torn along the dotted line, one might say.

Rivets, on a large sailing boat? Surely not. But, alas, yes. So often these days, constructional techniques owe more to manufacturing convenience than structural excellence. Usually, production yachts are constructed with the lid off — hull and deck being completed separately and joined at almost the last moment.

Whilst speeding up most other aspects of construction, this practise clearly makes that final vital integration of the hull and deck an exceedingly awkward business. Access will be difficult; and the notion of sending a man shambling into that plush pre-furnished interior with a bucket of resin and some chopped strand mat, is plainly out of the question. The only alternative, therefore, is some form of mechanical fastening — nuts and bolts or, God help us, pop rivets or self-tapping screws.

The most secure form of hull/deck joint is where the two mouldings have been fastened — preferably bolted — together and then substantially glassed over along the inside seam. With this sort of arrangement the entire hull/deck shell can be considered monocoque.

Next in our descending order of merit would be the bolted joint, with mastic or epoxy filler between the mating surfaces.

This can be an extremely strong and effective method — at best as strong as a glassed joint. Beware, however, the arrangement where the bolts also serve to hold the rub-rail in place. Should the rub-rail be ripped off — a not uncommon occurrence, by any means — then the bolts will be loosened and the joint would be insecure. Similar, but less vulnerable, would be a toe-rail fastened in the same manner.

That leaves the products of the Flip-top Boatbuilding Company. You don't need any advice on this. You'll recognise it when you see it and, no doubt, react in an appropriate fashion.

9 Steel

Building a steel yacht calls for more skill than the often relatively crude hull shapes would suggest. Welds shrink on cooling, causing distortion to the plating. Although this cannot be eliminated entirely, good techniques and a carefully planned approach to the sequence of construction can do a lot to minimise that 'hungry horse' look, where the plating appears sucked in between the frames.

As a matter of interest, hulls are usually plated up from mid-length, proceeding outwards towards the ends, and starting with the topsides — which for cosmetic reasons should be fairer. Welding should be kept to the minimum, so discontinuous welds on internal frames (Fig. 13) are a sign of good practise, not bad. Also, where possible, welds should not meet — though this is plainly unavoidable on the exterior plating where seam and butt welds must obviously come together at the corners. If you know what you are looking for, the internal arrangement of the welds can speak eloquently of the overall care taken.

Fair and shapely: Again, first stand back and observe the whole. For the reasons given above, you can expect to see some localised distortion, but try to ignore this and look for major variations in the sweetness of the lines. Pay particular attention to the chines and gunwales. Anywhere where two planes meet will test the accuracy of the lofting.

Many steel yachts are home built. Some are excellent, others are not. For the first time builder, skill usually advances with

Any general unfairness in the plating will be most obvious along the chines

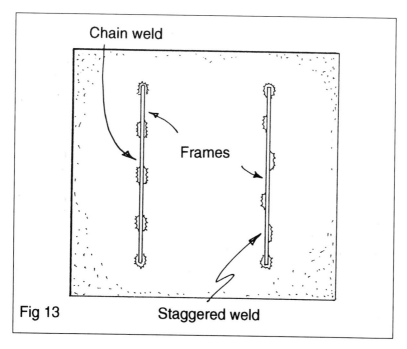

Fig 13

Chain weld

Frames

Staggered weld

experience. It's therefore an irony (and sometimes a downright pity) that the most demanding work — the lofting, the setting up of the frames, and the plating — takes place so early in the project.

Too fair to be true: In order to improve the appearance, some builders screed the topsides with fillers. Today these are usually epoxy/microballoon mixes, but concrete is sometimes used. If such fillers are intended to hide minor discrepancies in fairness, then their use is perfectly acceptable. But if thickly trowelled on to fill large hollows, this can lead to future problems. I once saw a magnificent steel yacht which had been involved in a fairly modest collision. The starboard side still gleamed like a grand piano, but the finish on the port topsides — the site of impact — had turned deciduous and much of it had fallen off.

A small magnet is a useful tool: first for detecting the presence of any filler, and then for judging its thickness. Obviously its 'pull' will be strongest when close to the steel, and will progressively weaken with distance. If the filler is very thick, little or no attraction will be felt. The little horseshoe magnet I carry in my survey kit will stick sufficiently well to a steel hull to support its own weight if the filler is about 4 mm or less. More than that and it will fall off.

Where located, patches of filler should be tapped to make sure they are adhering properly to the steel.

Rust — the red devil: Rusting is, of course, the oxidation of iron (which, as we all know, with some added carbon and other alloying constituents, makes steel). Unprotected metal in a marine environment can be expected to corrode away at a rate of up to 50 microns (0.002in) per annum.

Apart from the steel itself, the principal ingredients in this process are water and oxygen. In dry desert conditions rust is not a problem, and neither is it in the wet but totally airless depths of the ocean. Both Rommell's ruined tanks and the ill-fated *Titanic* share a related protection from rust, though stranded in vastly different circumstances.

This eternal preservation of the *Titanic* comes as something of a surprise to some people, who associate rusting simply with water, and reason that there's obviously lots of it in the Atlantic. They are similarly shocked when they discover that the underside of their steel yachts rust faster when laid up ashore in the rain than when immersed in the briny.

The factor they are ignoring, of course, is the part that oxygen plays. The most vulnerable areas of any steel structure are those exposed to both water *and* air. In the case of a boat, this means: topsides, decks and deckheads, bilges, and the band of hull just below the waterline which is well aerated by wave movement. And neither is the *quantity* of water important; a film of condensation will do every bit as much damage as several gallons sloshing around in the bilges.

Design detail is of the utmost importance. The conscientious builder will go to great lengths to eliminate pockets where water can gather — both above and below decks. Internally, limber holes should allow unimpeded drainage to the lowest point in the bilges. Where these are impracticable, any recesses should be filled with concrete so that puddles cannot form.

In some ways, the formation of rust can be likened to that of rot on a timber hull. The danger often lies in the less accessible areas where drainage and ventilation are poor, and maintenance awkward to sustain. Be prepared to crawl into the ends of the hull and to rely on your sense of touch to investigate those bits you cannot see. Feel under the side decks and cockpit seats and anywhere else you can reach. And if there is water in the bilge, do what you can to pump it dry.

If it's rusted then how much? Obviously, if you can see both sides of a component at once, then it's a simple matter to measure wastage. But the hull and deck plating, bulkheads, and tank sides are another matter. In days of yore, test holes would be drilled as required (and later plugged with rivets), but the modern surveyor uses ultrasonic gauges which are non-destructive, apart from the removal of small patches of paint.

Neither technique is appropriate to your provisional inspection. Once more you must rely upon your eyes. Steel doesn't rust uniformly, wearing away until paper thin all over. Invariably there are variations in the rates of wastage and these can often be seen as obvious surface irregularities. As illustrated by Figure 14 (p.70), a coincidence of what from each side might look like fairly innocuous pitting, may actually have eaten nearly all the way through — especially on thin plating.

Sometimes, almost invisible pinholes can betray themselves

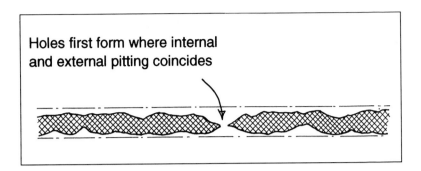

Fig. 14: Section through corroded metal plate.

by damp patches on dry antifouling, caused by bilge water leaking out from inside the hull.

Although true of all forms of construction, it is especially vital with steel that you have a surveyor give the hull the once-over before you commit yourself. Armed with his ultrasonic thickness gauge, he will be able to tell you how much metal remains in the various parts of the hull.

Thinned or pitted plating can usually be cut out and replaced. But, if corrosion is well advanced or has affected too many areas, it may be hardly worth the effort. Most people who have ever been involved in repairing steel boats will have been in the situation where they weld in one bit to find that the adjacent areas are also in dire condition — 'chasing the rust around the hull' as the expression goes.

Also, repairs can affect the way in which the stresses are absorbed within the structure. To butt a new, full thickness component against one wasted by corrosion, can cause stresses to be transferred to other weakened areas.

10 Aloft — Spars and Rigging _____

If you are lucky, the mast may be handily racked off at ground level so that you can examine its whole length, along with the halyards and the standing rigging. But it is more likely that you will find it stepped, and will have to resort to peering upwards to see as much of it as you can.

Binoculars are an excellent aid to mast gazing. Although

obviously not as convenient as having it all laid out before you, it's surprising how much you can see through the trusted 7 x 50's.

And later, should you eventually buy the yacht, then a detailed inspection of the whole mast would be sensible. Either pay to have it struck or go aloft in the bosun's chair. If the latter, then preferably use a halyard which actually passes through the top of the mast itself. I once ascended on a spinnaker halyard to find the swivel block at the masthead almost at the point of disintegration!

Hollow timber spars: These are glued up from shaped segments in a variety of different configurations. Very often scarfed (tapered) joints are also necessary to make up the required length. Such scarfs could be in the individual segments or (less likely) through the whole section of the mast.

Modern wooden spars are usually glued with epoxy or resorcinol resins — both of which form bonds stronger than the wood itself, and are virtually unaffected by ageing. However, earlier spar makers used relatively primitive glues which were neither as strong nor as long-lived as those available today. Some by now will have decided that they have done enough, and the joints will have surrendered completely.

So, look for splits along the glue lines. On varnished spars, the varnish can sometimes be seen lifting off along the joints — blatant evidence of movement and water penetration into the seam.

Split seams are difficult to repair on a piecemeal basis because it's almost impossible to clean out the accumulated dirt and old glue without opening the faces entirely. Simply squirting in more glue to fill an open crack won't do. Anyway, if a glue line has let go in one place, there's a good chance that other areas are also weakened. As a prospective purchaser, it's safer to think in terms of a new mast.

Ubiquitous alloy: The rather unlovely 'tin stick' — almost universal on production yachts since the sixties.

And in this particular application aluminium has proved to be a wonderful material. Compared to the crafted timber spar, or such exotic specialities as carbon fibre laminates, aluminium lends itself well to modern manufacturing techniques. Complex hollow shapes are extruded under immense pressures, and then heat-treated to enhance their strength. For added protection against corrosion the sections are usually anodised — an electrochemical process which increases the thickness and stability of the alloy's natural oxide film. If required, the anodic film can even be colour dyed for cosmetic effect — though this has become less popular recently.

Apart from the usual knocks and scratches, not a lot can go wrong with the actual section of such spars. Most problems relate to the fittings and their attachment.

Corrosion: Because aluminium's protective oxide film is fairly stable, and 'heals' if scratched away, most alloys are quite durable in the marine environment. It is when in contact with other metals that aluminium becomes vulnerable. Living as it does towards the 'least noble' end of the galvanic series (only cadmium, zinc, and magnesium suffer worse) it tends to be punished in favour of nobler metals where any galvanic action exists.

A common site for trouble is behind stainless steel fittings. Examine tangs, pad eyes, and spreader sockets for any build up of corrosion between faying surfaces. This will appear as a hard packed, rather crumbly, greyish-white powder. Sometimes this corrosion can have accumulated to the extent that the fitting base is actually distorted outwards.

Incredibly, even bronze based winches are sometimes found bolted directly against aluminium. The corrosion in these circumstances can be horrific.

Perhaps the only area where corrosion can lurk dangerously unseen, is where a mast extrusion has been spliced to increase its length. I once saw an instance when the owner of a keel-stepped mast (which could reasonably have been expected to stand unstayed) threw off all the rigging prior to having the stick lifted from her boat. Before she could yell 'Timber!', the mast pitched spectacularly over the stern, scattering the crew in a most entertaining manner. When the dust had settled, and we all had the opportunity to investigate this unexpected diversion, it was found that corrosion had weakened the internal sleeve at the splice, and it had consequently cracked right through.

But there isn't much you can do about such faults — apart

from fingering the worry beads. Happily, these incidents are almost rare enough to be discounted.

Corroded areas should be exposed. Where necessary, fittings should be removed from the mast and, if required, reinforcing plates fitted to repair any serious damage. When replacing these fittings, steps should be taken to insulate the stainless steel from the aluminium — either with zinc chromate paste, a suitable self-curing sealant, or a thin plastic membrane. I have seen cases where silicone sealant (which contains acetic acid) appears to have actually initiated corrosion so, personally, I never use it for this purpose.

Riggers' droop: Not to be confused with the brewers' variety, though there is some symptomatic similarity.

Spreaders should be trimmed slightly upwards to bisect the angle between the upper and lower spans of the cap shrouds (Fig. 15). Often, however, you will see them horizontal or — worse still — drooping like a *bandito's* moustache. Apart from the inherent insecurity of this arrangement, serious distortion — or even failure — of the spreader sockets can occur.

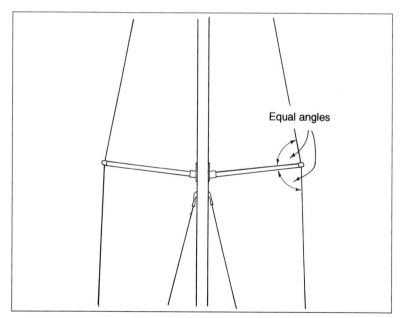

Equal angles

Fig. 15: Spreader alignment.

Dropped spreaders — a depressingly common sight. And, also on this ketch, the misalignment of the radar reflector renders it almost useless.

Seized sheaves: Masthead sheaves are not best placed for maintenance. Their life at the top of the mast is a lonely one, not exactly noted for regular attention.

Plastic or tufnol sheaves will often run for years without trouble, but aluminium sheaves can corrode and seize onto their axles. Partially or fully seized sheaves will soon wear asymmetrical, further diminishing their usefulness.

Untie the halyards and, with an end in each hand, pull them back and forth, testing for resistance. If the halyard won't shift at all, it will have jumped off the sheave and be jammed between it and the sheave box. This is more likely with wire halyards than rope.

The sinking mast step: This and the next section probably belong in another chapter, but, because they relate to the rig, I have included them here.

The compression loads imposed upon a conventionally stayed mast can amount to several tons — all of which concentrates at the foot. If the mast is stepped on deck — perhaps the commonest configuration on the modern sailing cruiser — then the internal structure must be designed to absorb these loads. An internal pillar (which often also supports the saloon table) or a strategically placed bulkhead are the most usual arrangements.

Get down on your hands and knees to see if the deck has dropped. And look for any cracks or other signs of movement both externally and internally. Frequently, this kind of damage is caused very early in a yacht's life and then stabilises, never to be a problem again. Consult your surveyor.

Chain plates

And, what presses down also pulls up. The compressive forces on the mast are matched by the tension in the shrouds, and the effect upon the structure is also reversed.

Again, this is a hands and knees job. Examine the chain plates for movement and look for any lifting of the deck. Touch is a reliable sense here. Sweep your hand along the deck and feel for any undulations. Crazing radiating from around the chain plates is always a bad sign.

As with the mast loads, movement may occur and then stabilise as all the 'slack' in the structure is taken up. However, and very unfortunately, many chain plate anchorages are fundamentally inadequate — sometimes relying on nothing more than just a couple of bolts through the deck itself, perhaps even without decent backing pads underneath. How so many builders fail to recognise the need for absolutely secure chain plates is a mystery to me.

If there is cause for suspicion above, investigate thoroughly below. This may not be as easy as it sounds. Like most of the deck gear on a GRP boat, the chain plates will probably have been fitted before the deck and hull were bonded together, and may now be concealed by a moulded deckhead liner or other furniture.

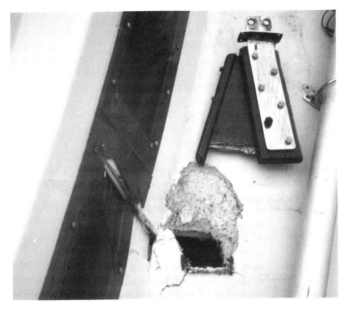

Chain plates are subjected to awesome loads. This one pulled right out through the deck, and brought a fair chunk of the bulkhead with it.

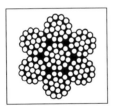

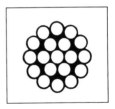

Fig 16   Fig 17

Wire ropes
The construction of steel wire ropes commonly used in yacht rigging are variously described as being 'one by nineteen', 'seven by seven' or 'six by nineteen'. This can cause confusion amongst the uninitiated, so a brief explanation might be in order.

The first number indicates the number of strands that make up the rope, and the second the number of individual wires within each strand. Hence, a 7 x 19 rope comprises seven strands, each of nineteen wires (Fig. 16), and a 1 x 19 is nineteen solid wire strands, configured as shown in Figure 17.

Obviously, the greater the number of wires contained within the total diameter of a rope, the thinner and more flexible these individual wires must be. It therefore follows that, for any given diameter, 6 x 19 rope (114 wires) is more flexible than 7 x 7 (49 wires), and that 1 x 19 (19 wires) is the most rigid. Arranged in terms of stretch resistance, the order would be reversed.

Typical uses aboard a yacht for each form of construction might be:

1 x 19	Standing rigging. Guardwires.
7 x 7	Running backstays. Tack pennants.
6 x 19 or 7 x 19	Halyards.

Although galvanised wire rope is still common on traditional type boats, the modern yacht is almost exclusively rigged with stainless steel. This presents the surveyor — whether professional or occasional — with a considerable problem. For stainless steel wire shows no conspicuous sign of mechanical distress right up to the time it fails. To assess it on its general shine would be like judging a politician by the width of his smile. There is no easy way of telling from the outside.

However, some clue can be gained by looking very closely at the point where the wire emerges from the terminals. Clean away any light rust that might have formed and look for flattened or shiny areas on the strands. If found, failure is close at hand.

Terminal condition — swages and eyes: Whereas all six and seven strand ropes can be satisfactorily hand spliced, this is not practicable with 1 x 19. To terminate 1 x 19, three distinct methods have been developed: roller (or hammer) swageing, where a tubular socket is squeezed on over the wire; the Talurit (or ferrule) method, where an eye is formed by pressing a copper collar around the wire; and mechanical terminals (Norseman or Sta-Lok), which are ingeniously engineered assemblies that can be fitted by hand with simple tools, and grip the wire with an arrangement of cones and compressing inserts.

Talurit swageing is reasonably successful in smaller wire diameters (say, to 5 mm maximum), but is not as satisfactory as roller swaged or Norseman type terminals. This is because stainless steel rope — particularly 1 x 19 — has little tolerance of the kind of severe deformation required to form the eyes.

That slit-eyed look: Elongation of Talurit eyes under tension further exacerbates this unwanted deformation. The thimble should be a fat heart shape — not stretched and pinched into a tight slit. So, compare the shape of the thimbles on the backstay — which is relatively lightly loaded — with those on the cap shrouds. If there is a marked difference, be warned.

And, while you are at it, look for parted strands on the crown of the eye. There is no margin of redundancy with stainless steel wire. Still having eighteen out of your nineteen strands intact is no cause for complacency. Whatever the circumstances, if a single strand has parted all are suspect. Replace the entire length — better still, all the standing rigging of similar age.

A Talurit swaged eye, distorted in service. A strand has already broken on the crown.

The Ten Year Rule: A well considered argument in yachting circles, opines that stainless steel rigging should be replaced at ten year intervals — especially if the boat has been hard used.

I agree. Regular replacement banishes doubt. Anyway, the cost of stainless steel wire rope would seem to have escaped the 'if it's boaty it's pricey' influence. It's one of the few items of marine hardware these days which actually impresses me by its value.

Split rings — the minuscule menace: As an alternative to the old fashioned and thoroughly reliable split pin (called a cotter pin in the U.S.), many yachtsmen use stainless steel split rings to secure their clevis pins.

To date, I know of four masts (one of which, I'm embarrassed to admit, was my own) which crashed down because of these awful little devices. The process is simple. First, the ring is snagged and partially straightened by a flogging rope; the foresheets are particularly adept at accomplishing this. Then, with the natural movement of the boat, the ring gradually rotates until it drops out of the clevis pin. The next stage in our nightmare scenario usually occurs to leeward. With no load on the shrouds, the clevis pin slides out. If this is not noticed by the crew (imagine it at night in lumpy conditions), the next tack sees the mast disappearing over the opposite side.

Of course, we all know that the clevis pins should be fitted with the heads inboard — easier to ensure on the lower fork of the rigging screw than on the rotating upper half. And taping over the rings would also add security. But neither of these are certain guarantees and, personally, I won't countenance split rings *anywhere* on the standing rigging or guardwires.

I put these points to a salesman on the stand of a recent marine trade show. 'Oh, we know there can be problems', he told me airily, 'but the yachtsmen find 'em convenient'. Speaking for myself, I don't find anything convenient about towing my mast astern.

Synthetic ropes

Another miracle of polymerisation, contrasting marvellously with the hairy coils of yester-year.

Sheets and halyards (when not of wire) are invariably of polyester. These are attacked by the ultra-violet rays from the sun, and will slowly degrade with use. However, this rate of

Disaster in the making. The split ring has been snagged by the foresheets and now could easily fall out.

degradation is quite slow and the ropes will probably have worn out anyway before weathering becomes a significant factor. But watch out if a boat has been left standing for a long time. In this case, ropes could be barely worn but badly weathered.

Polypropylene is another matter. This buoyant, often garishly coloured cordage suffers horribly in sunlight. The polypropylene net trampolines on a trimaran I once owned, had to be replaced after only a few months in the tropics. The first inkling that anything was amiss was when my leg plunged through.

Scratch the surface with your thumb-nail. If the fibres are severely degraded, they will be seen to break. If so, replace.

11 Sail Tales

It was off Mallorca during a classic boat rally. A large fleet of yachts was heading southwards towards Cabo Blanco. The three masted schooner *Creole* had just slipped by, and the Fifer *Altair* was fast overhauling us — both having started considerably later than ourselves, crewing aboard a handsome Laurent-Giles cutter of 1938 vintage. The wind had dropped to a torpid Force 2 and our speed was suffering disgracefully.

'I think the big genoa,' said George with satisfaction. The announcement carried the ring of inevitable annihilation for the opposition. Minutes later a mouldering bag was being heaved out through the forehatch, and we were hanking a distinctly elderly sail to the forestay.

'Looks a bit fragile', I observed.

'Sets like a dream,' said George. We laid back on the halyard and watched it fill.

Well, it did set like a dream (more or less), and for nearly half-an-hour at that. But then the wind unsportingly rose to a tempestuous Force 3, when the fabric chose to reduce itself into its component parts before our eyes.

'Don't understand it,' George gloomed, as we lowered the tatters to the deck. 'It was a nearly new sail when I bought the boat seventeen years ago. Wonder if I can have it mended.'

The moral to this is that some yachtsmen are not to be trusted when talking about their sails. It's not dishonesty that leads them astray, but sentiment. Sails are the wings of dreams. An otherwise quite clearsighted sailor will cling to an old sail as he might to some favourite jacket — nostalgia, rather than usefulness reserving its place in the wardrobe. Prompt any sailmaker and he will recount endless grisly stories of sails he has been asked to repair. 'You would think they'd know it was hopeless,' one told me, 'when they want you to patch the patches'.

And sails are expensive — usually a substantial proportion of the total value of a yacht. It behoves you, therefore, to inspect them as thoroughly as possible. Spread them out if practicable. If not, pull them from their bags, and examine the most critical parts as best you can within the confines of the boat.

Some damage will be obvious: Eyelets and cringles may be distorted or will have pulled out; luff wires may have rusted or frayed; piston hanks could be seized; and battens may have pushed out through the end of their pockets.

Chafe: The principal enemy. Wear can occur anywhere the sails touch the boat or rigging. On headsails, check along the foot where it passes over the pulpit or guardwires, and look for tell-tale soiled patches where it rubs against the spreader ends. Mainsails may bear against the caps or lower shrouds when running free. Fully battened mains are especially vulnerable.

Sails and sunlight: The bountiful sun, whilst great for tanning the torso, does absolutely no good at all to synthetic sailcloth. With every second of daylight the sails hang aloft, strength is gradually lost. And, unlike polyester cordage which is thick enough to be opaque, thin sailcloth is translucent and is being subjected to damage throughout its thickness.

Recently, UV resistant cloths have been developed which help to retard these ravages. An almost colourless protective coating is applied to the cloth during the calendaring process. This is claimed to extend the life of the sail by about 30% — or as much as 40% if the sail is also tan coloured. Naturally, it is important also to use treated thread.

Roller furling mains and genoas often have sacrificial strips sewn along the foot and leach. The amount of fading to these strips can be a useful pointer to age.

When inspecting sails, knowing something about the history of the boat can be helpful. For example, a single season's leisurely cruise in the Mediterranean might cause very little obvious wear, but the invisible UV degradation could be extreme.

Luckily the thread usually surrenders first. Give it the thumb-nail test and see how strong it still is. And be very wary of an ostensibly good sail which has been comprehensively overstitched.

The overall quality of the sails is something I always look for. Generous cloth weights for the size and purpose of each sail, substantial reinforcements around all corners and fittings, and good detailed work in the finishing, are all positive signs. The established sailmaker's enjoy (or otherwise) some variance in reputations. Ask around if you don't know already. Find his mark or label and judge by what you have learned of him. If there is no label at all (or any evidence of one which may possibly have become detached) then be very cautious. The better sailmakers are proud to put their names to their work. The worst may think it wiser not to.

Modern reefing — now you see it, now you don't: There are few items of equipment which have done as much to transform sailing as the roller furling gear. Complete sail control from the comfort of the cockpit has become a reality. Clambering forward to wedge yourself into the spray lashed pulpit has, for many of us, receded mercifully into dark memory. On our own boat, between weighing anchor in one place to dropping it again in another, we might never visit the foredeck at all.

But this convenience and contribution to safety has been gained at some cost. The humble piston hank might have been a pain to operate when you were cold and wet, but it very rarely let you down. Roller reefing, on the other hand, can be gloriously fallible.

Inspect the lower end for obvious damage. Look for corrosion to the aluminium — especially around any stainless steel components. Sometimes the ball bearings are visible; if so, check for broken or deformed balls. Rotate the foil extrusion by hand to see how easily it turns. If there is significant resistance, then the bottom of the gear could be clogged with an accretion of oxidised metal swarf and salt.

If the sail is bent on and conditions permit, actually test the gear in operation. But be very careful with the boat blocked off ashore in windy conditions. Once, in a crowded boatyard, the domino principle was dramatically demonstrated when the genoa suddenly filled and the boat sailed free of its shores.

I think this picture speaks for itself.

12 Deck Hardware

Although marine fittings are generally becoming more intricate, in mechanism terms they still remain fairly simple pieces of kit. If one doesn't work, it's usually pretty easy to see why. There are few tricks an unscrupulous vendor can pull to fool any buyer prepared to use his sight, touch, and common sense. Most diagnoses can be made simply by looking, cranking, pulling, or twiddling.

Ground tackle: The anchor should be large enough for the boat. Sometimes, if an owner is changing boats, the bower anchor might be taken ashore for future use, and the smaller kedge shackled on.

For general cruising, the following weights of 'patent' high-efficiency anchors (CQR, Bruce, Danforth, Delta et cetera) would be appropriate for each boat size LOA:

6m (20')	-	5 kg (11 lbs)
8m (26')	-	7.5 kg (16.5 lbs)
10m (33')	-	10 kg (22 lbs)
12m (39')	-	15 kg (33 lbs)
14m (46')	-	20 kg (44 lbs)
16m (52')	-	25 kg (55 lbs)

These should be thought of as the minimum. For serious offshore cruising or where exposed anchorages are anticipated, these weights should be substantially increased. Be wary of manufacturers' claims that lighter anchors will suffice — I know of no better aid to a good night's sleep than a hefty great lump of metal buried in the mud below you.

Rails, stanchions and guardwires: I have this fond memory of Arthur. He was a large man — very large, if truth be told — and the proud owner of a mid-sized cruising yacht. the two of us were enjoying a brisk sail down the coast in perfect summer conditions, supplementing our pleasure by sinking a few beers.

'Time to pump tanks, dear boy', Arthur said. Leaving me at the tiller, he clambered out onto the leeward side deck, wedged himself between the shrouds and guardwire, and proceeded to arrange the parts of his anatomy essential for the task.

With my gaze delicately averted from his poised form, I had the opportunity to actually see the guardwire lanyard aft stretch, strand, and then snap. From the side deck came a startled grunt followed by a considerable splash.

Going back for him was no problem, but getting him on deck proved very difficult indeed. Finally, using the boom and mainsheet as a derrick, I had him soggily aboard.

'My word,' Arthur gasped when he had recovered his breath, 'You could say I had my life in my hands there for a moment'.

Check that the pulpit, stern rail, and stanchions are secure. If there is excessive movement in the stanchion bases, have a look below to see if there are adequate backing pads.

The corrosion in cast aluminium bases can expand enough to actually split the socket. Pay particular attention to these.

The guardwire tensioning lanyards are out in all weathers and very subject to UV degradation. They cost pennies to renew, and there really is no excuse to let them deteriorate to the point where an Arthur could go swimming.

Examine the eye at the top of the stanchion for wear. If the cap is of aluminium or plastic, the guardwires can saw gradually inwards until they cut right through. Some people simply turn the stanchion so a new side is presented. This is absurd. To place the weakest side of the eye outboard is to make it less effective should a crew member fall against the guardwire.

Obviously, the whole system is of vital importance for crew safety. Any suspect components must be repaired or replaced immediately

Mooring cleats: Some older yachts still sport them but, alas, the trusted and sadly lamented samson post is virtually no more. These days you are much more likely to see dainty little aluminium mooring cleats which, whilst serviceable for more gentile purposes, often prove inadequate when the going gets really rugged. Too often, surveyors see signs of straining around the bases and, in the worst cases, gaping holes in the deck where the fitting has pulled completely out. Usually, the cause is simply that there are no proper backing plates under the deck to help disperse the loads.

The deck hardware on a modern GRP yacht is invariably fitted before deck and hull come together. This can sometimes make access to the fastenings below well nigh impossible. If a moulded deckhead liner is also fitted, so much the worse.

Winches and windlasses: To test, simply crank or wind as appropriate. Again, aluminium tends to suffer worse than bronze or stainless steel, so look especially carefully at these. Slip the chain off the windlass gypsy, and test both the winding mechanism and the clutch.

Where windlasses are fitted, there is often no other provision to make fast the chain. This is very poor practise. Windlasses are designed to wind, not to permanently secure. The surge and plunge of a yacht riding to anchor in exposed conditions can do damage to the windlass's innards.

All stiff devices should be stripped and serviced. If totally seized, then expect the worst. Winches and windlasses are often made of aluminium and bronze — hardly a good combination.

Hatches and windows: Most modern hatches are constructed of acrylic sheeting, set in either a thermo-plastic or a fabricated aluminium frame. Windows are usually toughened glass, acrylic, or polycarbonate, either fastened directly to the cabin sides or framed in aluminium.

On older boats, extruded rubber automobile type mountings can sometimes still be found. This is a deplorable arrangement, for which I have absolutely no affection. Rounding Dungeness against a westerly gale, I once spent several desperate minutes at a pump after a rubber mounted window was popped inwards by a wave.

Acrylic sheeting is yet another material affected by UV light. After a while it will start to craze, and this crazing will progressively worsen until there is significant structural impairment. The point at which it becomes unserviceable is a matter of judgement, and will be somewhat dependant upon the thickness of the sheeting, the size of the window, and the proposed purpose of the vessel.

Although not commonly used, polycarbonate sheeting is sometimes chosen for its immense strength (bullet proof screens in banks are made with it). However, it fogs badly in strong sunlight and, after a few years, will become almost opaque.

Aluminium surrounds can corrode. Unfortunately, most inter-screw fastenings (the flat dome headed nuts fitted on the inside of frames) are of chromed brass, which, of course, can react galvanically with aluminium. However, such corrosion is easily seen, and its severity can be readily assessed.

Look for signs of leakage. Smears of obviously non-original sealant are a sure giveaway. Leaks usually occur when sealing compounds or rubber gaskets harden and shrink. It may be possible to staunch them temporarily, but they are symptomatic of a general deterioration which will only get worse.

Repair of hatches and windows is seldom worthwhile. Almost always, replacement is the best and most cost-effective option.

13 The Nuts & Bolts_____

In a simpler era there was a straightforward division between sail and power. Power boats were filled with devices that roared, clanked, and made lots of smoke. Sailing boats were not — assuming we disregarded their skippers.

But these distinctions have become increasingly blurred. Although the size and number of engines might vary, sailboats are now almost as mechanically complex as motor boats. And the value of all this machinery has also risen. Whereas the replacement of some piddling little 5 hp yacht auxiliary might not have caused much pain, to change a modern diesel can easily set you back thousands.

It pays to try and make sure you get a good one.

Engine trials — the proof of the pudding: The modern marine diesel is an astonishingly durable piece of kit. The one in our yard launch looks like a ball of rust from the outside, but starts at the prod of a button, and will chug along all and every day without complaint.

Diesel auxiliaries tend to die of neglect, not overwork. Most are marinised versions of commercial engines which run for tens of thousands of hours in their shorebound guise. The typical boat auxiliary performs trifling tasks by comparison and, like many of us, is probably just too under-exercised to stay healthy.

Even power boat engines lead idle lives. No doubt constrained by high fuel costs, 70 hours a year is thought of as average, 200 positively epic. Again, compare that with any truck.

However, boat engines exist in an unsympathetic environment. Often awkward to maintain, with bilge water sloshing around their nether regions, they are more prey to corrosion from without, than wear from within.

Engine trials should be considered especially important if you're buying a power boat, where the value of the engines represents a very substantial proportion of the whole. And this means more than just starting them up whilst lying cosily alongside. Where practicable, the trial should be of sufficient length and duration for the boat to be run at full speed, and for the engines to reach their maximum service temperatures and oil pressures.

Rely on all your senses. Make sure the cooling water is pumping steadily. Listen for mechanical distress, feel for imbalance and excessive vibrations through your feet, and keep an eye on the gauges to see that all seems well. In twin engined craft look for disparities between them. If there is a calorifier plumbed into one engine, then it may run a little cooler than the other.

Try the gears in both forward and astern, listening for any nasty knocks as they engage. The controls should work smoothly, shifting between gears and applying power without surges or hesitation.

Finally, with the engine at its hottest, shut her down, open up the box and take a sniff of the beast. Smells are virtually impossible to describe but, I'm pretty certain, if the engine is over-cooked you will recognise the stench of scorched oil immediately.

Engine trials are never fool-proof — a rogue engine might still go undetected — but, short of dismantling it for inspection or conducting other sophisticated tests, there is no better way of assessing its condition than proving it in service. Also, it demands that an owner puts his own confidence in his boat on the line. Any foot-shuffling or other forms of prevarication should be viewed with deep distrust.

Smoke signals: An expert mechanic can tell quite a lot about a diesel from the colour of any exhaust smoke. All engines smoke when starting (actually, a lot of it is steam) but, when it has achieved its normal operating temperature, the exhaust should be virtually invisible. If it continues to belch forth smoke, then (amongst others) the following conclusions can be drawn by noting the colour of the smoke:

White — The fuel/air mixture is too lean. This may just need simple adjustment but could also be caused by air leaks in or around the inlet manifold.

Black — If the engine isn't under load, it indicates that the fuel/air mixture is too rich. The injection pump or the injectors themselves could be faulty. If the boat produces black smoke as the load increases, this would suggest that it's not achieving the revs it should for the amount of applied throttle — in other words, labouring. It could be that the boat is grossly over-propped (an oversized propeller or one of too coarse a pitch) or that the applied power is just too much for the hull — especially likely on a displacement boat limited by its hull speed. In the latter case, easing the throttle would eliminate the problem, but if the propeller is wrongly sized then obviously it must be replaced, reduced in diameter, or re-pitched.

Blue — This is probably caused by sump oil being combusted with the fuel. Worn rings, or burned valves may be to blame. If a turbo charger is fitted, then this could be defective.

Iron topsails — the sailboat auxiliary: If the boat is afloat when you first see her, then the opportunity to try her out under power should be easy — with, of course, the owner's consent. But, if she's laid up, then testing the engine in operation can be difficult — even impossible. Sometimes it's feasible to rig temporary cooling, so that the engine can be run briefly, by diverting the water intake to a bucket; but, again, you would need the nod from the owner. And make sure the boat is shored up really securely. If the vibration shakes the wedges loose, the results could be catastrophic.

Check the external condition of the engine, looking for any obvious defects. Localised areas of rust on an otherwise clean block could point to a blown gasket or other cooling water leak.

Examine the engine mounts and bearers to make sure these are secure. Rocking the engine from side to side by hand can sometimes reveal problems here. Half casually, not expecting any results, I once did this to my own engine to find that one of the aft mounts had collapsed completely and another was crumbling under the inherited strain.

Pay particular attention to belts and hoses. More engines are destroyed by overheating following cooling water failure than for any other reason. Synthetic rubbers usually start to crack before bursting completely. Often this can best be seen at the ends, where the hose clips have bitten in.

If the engine has a hand start, ship the handle, open the decompression levers, make sure the engine is in neutral, and give it a turn. Then close the levers and attempt to swing it carefully against its compression. Carefully, mind! Remember, you don't have to close an ignition switch to start a diesel.

Fuel tanks and pipelines: Fuel tanks are usually stuffed into spaces not useful for other purposes. Consequently, they can often be rather inaccessible. Inspection is invariably limited to the outside — and often you won't even be able to see very much of that.

For petrol engines, tanks should be made of galvanised steel, brass, or internally tinned copper. Diesel tanks can be made of plain steel (not galvanised), stainless steel, or GRP. Copper, brass, or galvanised steel tanks are *not* acceptable because they react chemically with diesel fuel.

Pipelines should be in seamless copper or stainless steel, with the shortest possible flexible 'tail' at the engine end to absorb vibration. Preferably there should be a pre-filter fitted as close to the engine as possible to sift out any abrasive particles which might damage the injection mechanism.

Plastic piping — used mainly for its convenience and low cost — is a poor substitute, and will probably be rejected by the surveyor for safety reasons. The argument goes that in the event of a fire it could melt, flooding the boat with fuel. But, if the tank is situated very close to the engine, it may be judged safer to use continuous short lengths of flameproof flexible hose, rather than introduce unnecessary joins which could leak.

Propellers: Unless fitted as part of a stern drive unit, nearly all propellers are made of bronze — simply speaking an alloy principally of copper and tin. Unfortunately, for the unwary, the word 'bronze' covers a wide range of such alloys, the various characteristics of which are not always understood.

For less demanding applications, involving low speeds and modest power (sailboats, displacement cruisers, et cetera*)*, *manganese* bronze is often chosen for reasons of economy. But manganese bronze isn't really a bronze at all, but a form of *brass.* It contains a high percentage of zinc which, when acting galvanically with the copper, results in the less noble metal's depletion. The copper remains, porous and seriously weakened. This process is known as *dezincification.*

So, carefully scrape back to bare metal and take a look. If you can see pronounced pink patches, typically a little lower than the surrounding metal, then the prop is of manganese bronze and it has already started to dezincify. In severe cases the blade will be heavily pitted and you'll be in no doubt whatsoever. And look at the thin edges and tips of each blade. Often, when dezincification is still not well advanced, you can actually crumble away small bits of metal with nothing more hostile than your finger-nail.

Before moving on, it's worth saying something about the alternatives. *Aluminium* bronze is a vastly preferable alloy. It costs about 30% more than manganese bronze but is of superior strength and is unaffected by dezincification — in the long term, generally better value overall. Being stronger, it's the first choice for high speed or folding propellers, anyway. It makes just as much sense on a cruising boat.

Shafts: Although bronze or monel shafts are occasionally seen, the most common material used today is stainless steel (usually of 316 Grade).

Wear occurs at all points of contact between the shaft and its various bearings and glands. As these worn areas hide rather cravenly inside the fittings, they are difficult to inspect without first drawing the shaft. But, luckily, the flexible engine mounts allow some fore-and-aft movement with propeller thrust and, sometimes, the wear can extend a little way along the shaft to where it can just be seen. Examine all points where the shaft emerges. If possible, measure their diameter with vernier callipers and compare it with an obviously unworn section.

Crevice corrosion: This is a rather peculiar form of galvanic corrosion caused by an 'oxygen .differential' between adjacent areas of the same metal, which causes it to behave like dissimilar metals. Stainless steel can be seriously attacked by it — particularly around the propeller where the extreme turbulence can produce abnormal aeration of the water.

Often also called 'pitting corrosion', this phrase describes it well. Small, deep cavities can eat into the prop shaft with alarming rapidity, reducing it to a hollow shadow of its former self within a few months. Again, check the shaft where it emerges from the various fittings.

Molybdenum bearing stainless steels such as 316 are resistant to crevice corrosion but are by no means totally immune.

Corrosion in its various forms often occurs unseen. The propeller shaft has severe crevice corrosion, the iron keel bolt has simply rusted away, and the bronze fastening on the left is dezincified and extremely brittle.

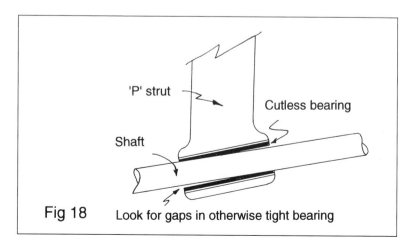

'P' strut

Cutless bearing

Shaft

Fig 18   Look for gaps in otherwise tight bearing

Cutless bearings: These are water lubricated, fluted rubber bearings, contained in a tubular bronze or phenolic laminate shell.

Check cutless bearings for wear by moving the shaft from side to side. Some slack can be expected, but if it's excessive, the bearing should be replaced. Exactly what 'excessive' means is open to interpretation, but don't fret about it too much. Cutless bearings are accommodating things which can be abused horribly and still function.

Shaft alignment: If the cutless bearing is carried in a P strut, and you can therefore see both ends of it, you should check that the axial alignment of the shaft is concentric with that of the bearing (Fig. 18, p.93).

If misalignment is found, the shaft/engine coupling should be separated, the shaft re-aligned, and the engine mounts adjusted accordingly.

Stern drives: These are complicated assemblies which, without benefit of X-Ray vision, are difficult to check *in situ*. But definitely give it the once-over for corrosion. Check the integral anodes (usually a ring anode just forward of the propeller boss, and a bar anode elsewhere). If these are totally depleted then the chances of galvanic corrosion are high.

Take a close look at the rubber bellows which covers the drive shaft constant velocity joint. If this is split, fear some rather expensive damage inside.

If the batteries are aboard, it may be possible to activate the tilt mechanism. The steering is usually entirely manual — either by Bowden cable or hydraulic — and should be testable simply by turning the wheel. And whilst you're at it, make sure that the reversing (I thought boats went 'astern') lock is working. Put the gear lever astern, grab the unit by the propeller, and try to lift it upwards. If you can it isn't, and if you can't it is. Also give it a bit of a shake from side to side to check for general wear.

But the best advice is to be generally cautious about stern drive units. Inherent engineering complexity and dubious combinations of metals make them awfully fallible. Servicing them is labour intensive and the manufacturers have never been exactly bashful about charging top rate for the bits. If you see one which seems in poor condition, then believe that it's probably *worse* than it looks until someone can prove to you otherwise.

Trim tabs: The adjustable variety are usually worked by an electrically driven hydraulic ram, controlled by a switch at the steering position. The tab surface itself is usually of stainless steel.

Check the unit in operation and the tab for signs of corrosion. Look especially around the hinges, for any sign of crevice corrosion or any cracking or other structural problems. Examine the hoses and rams as best you can to see if they are sound.

14 Sparks — The Electrics & Electronics

On *Whisky Jack*, the trimaran I sailed to Texas in 1974, the only electrics aboard were a domestic type radio receiver, a hand held RDF set, a Callbuoy emergency radio, and a flashlight — all of which were powered by internal batteries. With no inboard engine, and such exotic gear as solar panels only just becoming available (at prohibitively expensive prices), I didn't have the charging capacity for anything more sophisticated. Even the cabin and navigation lights were paraffin, such was the simplicity of this lightweight flyer.

But now, personally older and fatter and more accustomed to convenience, I own a boat which, at least so far as navigation aids are concerned, would have made a merchantman envious three decades ago. Marine electronics have advanced almost beyond recognition. Solid state circuitry has allowed extraordinary developments. Tiny bits of kit now perform prodigious feats of computation with remarkable reliability. And the understandable demand for all this wizardry has created a large and vigorous market in which the manufacturers are obliged to compete rather hard. To our collective satisfaction and gain, we yachtsmen have seen quality rise and prices fall — perhaps the only instance of this to be found in boating as a whole.

But although relative prices have tumbled, most electrical and electronic equipment still lives firmly in arm-and-a-leg territory. The prospective purchaser has an obvious interest in its condition for, if defective, its replacement costs could easily add many, many hundreds of pounds to the cost of a second-hand boat.

But first the basic electrics.

Batteries: The heart of the whole system. These should be of good capacity and, on a sailing boat, of the 'deep cycling' type — sometimes, not quite correctly, known as *traction* batteries. Your average car battery is designed only to deliver a large belt of power to start the engine, and thereafter to be continuously topped up by the alternator. Vehicle type batteries might just be acceptable on a power boat, where comparable conditions exist, but would be quite unsuitable for a sailboat which must tolerate severe depletion between opportunities to charge. Dedicated marine batteries are now commonly available, so only penny-pinching would lead someone to fit anything else.

The proof of a battery is obviously its ability to hold its charge. And there are only a few things you can do to determine this by casual inspection. If you can unscrew the filler caps, peer inside to check the level of the electrolyte. If it is very low then obviously there has been neglect. Also try to see if the plates are buckled. If they are, you can be sure this battery is past redemption.

If you're lucky, a voltmeter may be fitted to the boat, which will instantly allow you to judge its charge state. If not, the brightness of the cabin lights may give you some indication. Turn them all on — and the navigation lights, for good measure — to see how the batteries cope under load. And, if there is more than one battery, select them in turn, watching for variations in intensity.

If a battery is found to be very flat, then for pricing purposes assume that it's ruined — even if of a deep cycling type. Prolonged discharge will seriously impair a battery's functional capacity. If it's been left over a winter, slowly ebbing away, then you can bet it's in poor shape.

Loom without a view — a current idiocy: In the chintzier

reaches of interior design, electrical wiring is considered to be unsightly stuff, to be buried away beyond our delicate gaze. Aesthetically this might have merit, but for the purposes of inspection and maintenance, it makes about as much sense as welding shut the bonnet of your car.

Yacht surveyors aren't often asked to perform exorcisms, but I was once called upon to investigate 'mysterious noises from above' — meaning the deckhead. Sure enough, with the boat on its mooring, I didn't have to listen hard to detect a dry and rhythmic sound; no doubt a spectral mariner dragging his wounded body along the side decks. Actually, it turned out to be the wiring for the cabin lighting, installed loosely between the moulded GRP deckhead liner and the deck, and now scraping back and forth with the natural rocking of the boat. We managed to extract some of it for inspection and were horrified to see that in many places the insulation had worn right through.

So, examine the physical condition of the wiring as best you can. Look for connections which might be corroded. The pulpit mounted bicolour light circuit is especially vulnerable, typically being led through the chain locker.

Large is beautiful: A common misapprehension about boat electrics centres on the erroneous belief that, because low voltages are involved, the wiring itself can be of small diameter. The reverse is actually the case. Low voltages require high amperages for any given power output (wattage). And it is the *amperage* that determines the size of wire that should be used.

To illustrate this, let's assume a 24 watt navigation light. At 12 volts this would draw 2 amps, at 24 volts only 1 amp, and at 240 volts (if this were practical) just a measly one-tenth of an amp.

On many boats the original circuits will have been extended to support extra equipment put aboard. Often these improvised hook-ups will have been done in ignorance, perhaps connecting to circuits already fully loaded, or using wire of just too light a diameter for the task. Sometimes connections are made directly to the battery without any fuse protection.

The resistance caused by an inadequate conductor will result in a voltage drop, possibly affecting the proper working of equipment. An example might be a navigation light, situated a fair distance from the batteries, reduced to non-compliance with mandatory regulations by nothing more than a strangled electrical supply. Electronic navigational gear is particularly sensitive. Some will switch themselves off rather than risk delivering false readings.

If the circuit is grossly overloaded, it can also run hot, gradually breaking down the insulation to the point where a dead short could occur. A fire at sea is not a cosy prospect.

Making the connection: Of course, no matter how good all the conductors may be, they're no earthly good unless joined together properly. Chocolate block type connectors are favoured by many boatbuilders for their low cost and easy installation. But, although undoubtedly convenient, these troublesome little gadgets seem to have a special attraction for corrosion.

Personally, if I find one, I like to give the wire a gentle little tug to see how securely the connection is made.

Switches and fuses: Operate all switches to see if they work. Feel for any stiffness which could indicate internal corrosion. The rotating lens type of cabin lights are notoriously unreliable. If you have to fiddle with one to make an emphatic contact, then the unit needs replacing. And pull a couple of fuses, again checking the metal parts for corrosion.

Piecemeal repair of defective circuitry is rarely satisfactory. Problems of deterioration in one area must cast suspicion over the entire installation. The marine environment is tough on all things electrical and it's unreasonable to expect them to last for ever. There comes a point where the most sensible plan is to rip it all out and start again. In my opinion, bearing in mind the fire risks, this point occurs a good deal earlier than many people recognise.

Electronics: The microcircuitous workings of these magical toys is hidden to view, so we can do little else but turn them on and see if they work.

Obviously, the information they then deliver must reflect the particular circumstances of the day, and it's helpful to know what to expect. For instance, if it's blowing a lusty Force 6 from the East and the wind indicator shows a feeble 2 from South, then obviously something is amiss. Likewise if the Decca believes you to be in Bagshot when you're actually in Burnham, then this is a sick piece of kit. So don't just switch them on and admire the little numbers. Take the trouble to know your latitude and longitude (within reasonable limits of accuracy) in advance. Compare the readings with reality and make sure they match.

Some equipment can't be tested properly with the vessel ashore, so you may have to take a chance. But it may be possible to spin a log impeller (or have a friend do it for you) to ensure there is some sort of response on the display. The activity of echo-sounders can be checked by holding a small portable radio, tuned to an AM band, near the transducer. The clicking sound will confirm that the pulses are being transmitted.

15 The Comforts of Home

The domestic trappings that make up the interior are often overlooked — perhaps dismissed as being merely landlubberly accessories to the boat proper, hardly worth the same sort of serious attention. Considering their collective value, this can be an expensive mistake. Totting up the costs of outfitting our own boat, *Spook*, I was surprised and a little embarrassed to find that we had spent more on the homey trimmings than we had on the sails. The berth cushions alone were worth more than the mainsail and genoa combined.

Upholstery: Many production boats use cheap foam inserts which compress with age. So give them the bum test and see how they feel. Nothing can be done to resuscitate them once they are past their prime. And if you can face it, give them a sniff. Successively dampened cushions can take on a less than entrancing pong after a few years' hard use.

And, if you are budgeting for replacement, then for heaven's sake go for a fire-resistant grade. Being marooned on a smouldering boat whilst hydrogen cyanide takes over the cabin is dodgy in the extreme.

The loo: Another fun job. With the vessel afloat, testing is easy. With it ashore you can do little more than operate the various handles, inspect the hoses and seacocks, and have a stab at guessing at the condition of its innards.

Cooker and gas installation: Once, many lifetimes ago, I nearly became the first Briton in orbit. We were halfway across the Channel in a borrowed boat. Cherbourg beckoned with its restaurants and duty-frees. The weather was warm and mild, we had sunk a couple of beers for lunch and, as appropriate on such occasions, I was passing an afternoon watch below surveying the deckhead with my eyes closed. Stranded between sleep and wakefulness, I was drifting off ever deeper when there was a shout from the cockpit.

'Andrew! D'you smell gas?'

Gas? Damn the fellow for his asinine jokes. But then, as my senses returned fully, the stench in my nostrils banished all thoughts of humour. The cabin was filling with butane, surely now already at a sufficient concentration to be explosive. Stumbling about the cabin, rapidly becoming sickened with both fumes and fright, I sought to find the leak. On deck I could hear my companion yanking out the contents of a cockpit locker, struggling to gain access to the gas cylinder stowed somewhere in its depths.

Well, we didn't explode, but it was a sobering few minutes, I can tell you. With the gas turned off, and the cabin vented, we eventually traced the fault to behind the cooker. It was large, heavy, and extremely primitive. It was also gimballed and it was its swing on these gimbals which had done the damage. Heeled on starboard tack, the base of the cooker had repeatedly hammered into the copper gas pipe until it had fractured.

Of course, the whole installation was a disaster waiting to happen. The cylinder was stowed inaccessibly in an unvented locker also stuffed with other gear. No shut-off cocks were readily to hand in case of emergencies. And, as we discovered, the run of the pipework made it inherently vulnerable to damage.

The terrible dangers associated with gas are well known to all of us, and yet a horrifying number of dangerous installations remain. Figure 19 shows schematically an ideal arrangement.

Although sometimes not practicable on every boat, as far as is possible, every feature should be adopted.

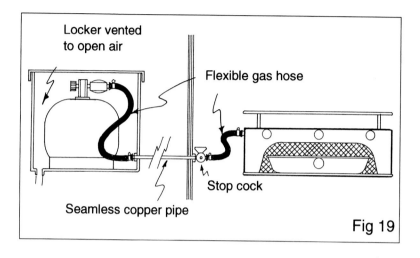

Fig 19

16 Buying

Having done the homework, worn out the shoe leather, and satisfied yourself that what you've found should suit you very nicely, the time will eventually come to consummate the deal. Now you must start talking serious money — either with the broker, who will pass on your offers, or with the owner directly if no broker is involved.

The sequence of events should then unfold something like this:

The initial bargaining: This will occur before either party is committed in any way and is, perhaps, the most vital part of the whole transaction.

Don't be too timid in your opening bid. No doubt the money you have in your pocket didn't come your way easily, and there's no reason why you should now part with more of it than you have to. No matter how genteel you might wish it to be, bargaining is essentially an adversarial encounter, where each party hopes to emerge with the largest share of the cake.

So, be bold. Put your finer instincts behind you and pitch your offer substantially below the asking price. No right-minded vendor expects to get all that he asks for, and you may be astonished to find that your offer is instantly accepted — in which case you will probably kick yourself for not bidding lower.

However, in this first sparring it is rather more likely that your offer will be declined — perhaps with some umbrage if it was insultingly low. But in this refusal may lie some indication of the kind of money the owner *really* expects to receive. He may even come right out and tell you. Either way, you can then reconsider your position and decide whether to up your offer, or back off from the deal to trawl in other waters.

But *always* take the trouble to negotiate the very best price you can at the outset. Some people prefer to wait until after the survey, which is a mistake. We shall discuss this in the later section on 'The undisclosed defect'.

Sales agreements and deposits — the brokerage route: So, now you have agreed a price, shaken hands on it, and the time to start wrapping up the deal is nigh. If a professional yacht broker is involved, he will steer you through the paperwork from here on.

First, a Sales Agreement should be signed by yourself and the vendor. A deposit (usually 10% of the purchase price) is then paid to the broker, who will hold it on his client's behalf. This deposit is returnable to you if the transaction founders for legitimate reasons (which we will discuss later), but could be lost if you renege frivolously. The protection you gain is that the boat will be withdrawn from the market and not offered to anyone else until your negotiations either finalise or fail.

Typically, such sales agreements will give you a stipulated time slot in which to have the vessel surveyed, and a further period beyond that (usually 15 days) to come up with the balance of the money if everything proves satisfactory. These periods can be extended by mutual assent.

Private deals: Although informal transfers of ownership can be concluded both amicably and successfully, some go horribly wrong. I have known occasions when decent and well-meaning people have come near to blows because each held a slightly different perspective of what precisely had been agreed.

The best types of understandings are those *where there can be no misunderstandings*. This means that every aspect of the negotiations should be recorded in writing — the agreed price, the inventory, the schedule of payments, and any other relevant terms or conditions. Both parties should retain copies of these memorandums so that, in the event of dispute, they can be referred to for clarification. If you find that the vendor is reluctant to participate in this pernickety approach, then do what you can to keep your own notes of all dealings.

But by far the safest procedure is to use a standard sales agreement, such as that available from the Royal Yachting Association, RYA House, Romsey Road, Eastleigh, Hampshire SO5 4YA. This form is very similar in substance to that used by most brokers, and provides a solid legal framework in which to buy your boat. Its use is strongly recommended.

Surveys and surveyors — *do you need them?* The short and emphatic answer is 'yes', to which follows naturally the question 'why?'.

The primary purpose of your own inspection of the boat was to seek out the more obvious defects before you got involved in major expense. But, no matter how diligently you went about this, your personal assessment will still fall short of the kind of detailed evaluation that a surveyor could provide. And, remember that your opinion is by no means objective. You, after all, are sufficiently deranged to want to buy a boat in the first place. Love is blind, as we all should know.

The purposes of a survey are fourfold:

a) To ensure that you are not buying an outright wreck. Hopefully, in broad terms, you will have already established this for yourself, but it's still important to have a professional opinion.

b) To advise you of any aspects of the vessel's condition which might be a threat to safety. Here the surveyor's experienced eye might pick up small but crucial details you could have missed.

c) To list any defects and advise on the likely costs of repair. As any sales agreement should include the vital phrase 'subject to survey', the surveyor's report then becomes a powerful instrument for re-negotiating an appropriate downward adjustment in price. Remember that even a boat in very run down condition can be an excellent buy if you can get it for the right money.

d) To provide the kind of independent assessment of condition and value which could be required by insurance or finance companies. This is particularly important if the boat is more than ten years old. Often, after boats have been bought without a survey, the new owner then finds that one is required before he can insure it. In some very unfortunate cases, the surveyor then discovers serious defects which would have ruled the purchase out in the first place, or at least forced a substantial reduction in price. And a final word of warning: being a habitually cautious bunch, insurers will usually only accept reports from 'qualified' surveyors. The opinion of your local pundit who will 'knock you out a survey for a couple of pints' might be stuffed to the brim with maritime wisdom, but will be firmly rejected when tendered with your proposal form.

The qualified yacht surveyor — who is he?: The total number of surveyors active throughout Britain isn't much more than a hundred; hardly demanding a formal, academically structured route into the profession — though many have backgrounds in naval architecture and the world of big ships. But, at the end of the day, anybody can become a yacht surveyor simply by proclaiming himself one. So how can you be sure of his credentials?

The professional yacht surveyor earns his qualification by experience, and his living by examining boats and reporting upon their condition in a factual and impartial manner. During the course of a year he pokes his way through hundreds of different boats, delving into places sometimes rarely, if ever, seen even by their owners. The professional surveyor probably sees more boats in greater detail in a single season than most yachtsman will see in a lifetime.

In 1912 the Yacht Brokers Association was founded and rapidly grew to embrace the closely related professions of yacht designing and surveying. Now known as the *'Yacht Brokers, Designers and Surveyors Association'* (more handily, the YBDSA), it is the *only* association of its type in Britain, and its membership is restricted to individuals rather than companies.

Applicants for membership of the YBDSA must first have had

many years experience in the boating industry. All are carefully vetted before acceptance. In such a relatively small profession, all are already known to the established practitioners, and letters of approval and support are sought. Even after election, most are required to serve a three year probationary period before they can publicly declare their membership or use the YBDSA emblem in their advertisements or letterheads. All members are required to carry substantial *Professional Indemnity Insurance* for the protection of their clients, and are obliged to abide by a strict *Code of Practice* which ensures the highest ethical standards.

So, before you engage a surveyor, it makes sense to ask him if he's a member of the YBDSA. After all, at the end of the day you are simply buying a man's professional opinion. And it's reassuring to know that this opinion is acknowledged and respected by the boating industry at large.

Beware the 'Broker's Friend': Where possible, choose your own surveyor. Never unquestioningly allow the vendor or his broker to appoint one for you. As in all professions, there are variations in competency and conscientiousness — and also, regrettably, the occasional rotten apple.

It's clearly in the vendor's interest to have his boat inspected by a 'soft' surveyor who may not be quite as stringent as the next. The unscrupulous may try to contrive this.

On request, brokers will present a list of local surveyors, from which you can choose. Most will then leave you to make your selection without further influence. But you might find yourself gently led: 'They're all much of a muchness, sir, but personally we've always found this chap here very helpful'. Be careful. Sellers and buyers can have very different understandings of the word 'helpful'. Good advice is one thing, but if you feel you are being unduly pressured, proceed with caution and make your own enquiries.

The specialist surveyor: The ubiquitous GRP yacht is bread and butter to most surveyors, but certain types and construction may be outside every individual's experience. For example, the younger surveyor brought up with modern construction methods may be (but by no means necessarily) less hot on timber vessels. Conversely, an older man who served his time amongst the wood shavings of a traditional yard might be less confident inspecting one of today's lightweight flyers, built of space-age materials.

If there is anything unusual about the boat you're proposing to buy, satisfy yourself that your surveyor is fully conversant with the type. A responsible surveyor (who, after all, has his reputation on the line) would, anyway, decline to survey a boat he was unsure about. But it does no harm to ask him

The undisclosed defect: Now, with the surveyor's report in your hand, it may be appropriate to invoke the 'subject to survey clause' to your advantage.

If significant defects, which were not declared at the time the initial purchase price was agreed, later come to light in the survey, you have grounds to negotiate a further reduction in that price. The word 'significant' is open to interpretation, but obviously excludes trivial defects of purely cosmetic importance.

This introduces an interesting moral element. What if, during your own inspection of the boat, you had spotted something detrimental that the owner hadn't told you about? Should you have drawn it to his attention and included it in your general negotiating campaign at that time, or would it have been smarter to have kept it to yourself, waited until it inevitably appeared in the surveyor's report, and then used it as a stick to beat the price down more, feigning bitter disappointment at this 'unexpected' news? I leave this to your own conscience but, in my opinion, it is nearly always better at first to be vague about the condition of the boat (though not about the inventory) leaving your tactical options open and the detailed nit-picking until the later stages. Of course, if the vendor deliberately conceals a major defect from you, then he has only himself to blame when his deceit comes back to haunt him.

Earlier, we touched upon the importance of negotiating hard from that very first skirmish before the survey. Not to do so is to surrender ground that you will never regain.

To illustrate why, let's take as an example a yacht offered for sale at ten thousand. You've been for a sail, looked it over closely, and have warmed to both it and the owner, who seems the kind of chap who will treat you right. Being refined sort of gents, to whom haggling is distasteful, both of you mutually agree to defer your negotiations until the results of the survey are known. In due course the surveyor does his stuff and comes up with a list of recommendations which, say, will cost about a thousand. The vendor magnanimously agrees to drop the price by that amount and you uneasily accept.

Of course, this is a terrible deal for you. The asking price almost certainly had a negotiating buffer built in — plus a bit more for contingencies — and that buffer is still contained within the agreed sum. If, say, you had initially negotiated down to *nine-and-a-half* thousand instead, your position to negotiate further on the basis of undisclosed defects would have been no less strong, and the owner would probably still have had to drop his price accordingly.

And, of course, there is also some risk that the surveyor's report will read like a glowing eulogy in praise of perfection, in which case you will have absolutely no grounds whatsoever for further bargaining and will be stuck with paying the asking price in full.

As every accomplished haggler knows, a man will accept by degrees what he could never swallow whole.

No offers? — No way!: As a surveyor, I often hear from my clients that the vendor has stipulated that the price is firm, regardless of anything my survey might unearth. I tell them to smile sweetly and ignore such blustering. No price is ever firm until the final deal is struck. If significant defects come to light they can *always* form the basis of further bargaining, should the buyer choose to pursue it.

All boats have a realistic market value — warts and all. If new warts are discovered, then obviously the value drops. The vendor has to accept this or withdraw his boat from sale. So, *never* enter into an agreement wherein you waive your rights to negotiate.

Defects, sir? — Don't worry about a thing!: The vendor is not the man to take care of any necessary repairs. With the price agreed, anything he spends from thereon is lost money. The impulse to skimp on the job will be extreme.

It's better by far to negotiate an adjustment in price and then have the job done yourself. That way you have both control over the repairs and protection under the Sale of Goods Act should things go wrong.

Ownership — *is it actually his to sell?:* This can be a tricky area, fraught with potential doubts. How can you be sure that the yacht hasn't been stolen, or hasn't a hefty mortgage outstanding against it?

If the vessel is currently registered as a British Ship under Part 1 of the Merchant Shipping Act 1894 (hereafter referred to as 'Part 1'), then the ownership and any outstanding mortgages or other liens will be recorded by the Registrar of Shipping. A transcript of these details can be obtained from the Registrar at the main Port of Registry for that vessel for a fee — currently £25. Alternatively, and assuming that this is convenient, you can inspect the register in person for £10. The 'main' Port of Registry is, incidentally, the administrative centre for a group of lesser ports. Quite naturally, it is usually the largest port in each area.

Since 1983 there has been an alternative to full Part 1 registration. This is the Small Ships Register (usually abbreviated as SSR), which was ably administered on behalf of the government by the Royal Yachting Association until June 1992. Then, following, tenders from other organisations, the responsibility for its administrations was switched to the government's own Driver & Vehicle Licensing Agency. Their address is: Small Ships Register, DVLA, Swansea, SA99 1BX.

Unlike the Part 1 Register, the SSR is not a register of *title*, and cannot therefore be regarded as any proof of ownership. The registration document itself is in some ways similar to the log-book of a car, which simply records the 'keeper' of the vessel. Also, marine mortgages cannot be recorded against the SSR. If lenders require this kind of security, then a vessel must be registered under Part 1.

So, what are the practical implications to the prospective purchaser of a boat registered under the SSR? Although the SSR document is not absolute proof of ownership, if a vessel is used for purely private purposes, then it's very likely that the holder and owner are the same. Certainly, if a boat displays an SSR number, and the vendor can't produce the supporting documents, then this would be cause for suspicion.

Other clues may provide additional, if still not conclusive, evidence of ownership. Bills of Sale, insurance papers, old survey reports, receipts for repairs or mooring fees, yacht club memberships, and even the boat's log book can all point to the vendor's legitimate association with the craft.

And, at least you'll know that under the SSR no loan company can have a mortgage on the boat. The only liens that could be outstanding would fall into the following categories:

1)   A *possessory* lien is the right to retain a boat until specific charges in respect of it have been paid off. For instance, a repairer, a marina, or a salvage operator has the right to hang on to the boat until his rightful bills are settled. Should he lose possession (unless fraudulently) the lien is not revived by the creditor snatching it back.

2)   A *statutory* lien covers stores or equipment which are delivered to a boat. In these cases the vessel itself can be sued and arrested.

3)   A *maritime* lien is, perhaps, the most ominous trap a purchaser should be wary of. This form of lien arises from claims for salvage, or a claim for damages caused by the vessel, and follows the vessel even when it's sold by the owner in whose hands the liability arose. A Bill of Sale presented by the vendor to you which includes the protective phrase 'free from all encumbrances, debts, liens and the like' would not erase this liability. The Courts could still arrest and, if appropriate, order the sale of the vessel.

Of, course, it's almost impossible to determine beyond doubt that the apple isn't wormier than it seems, but you can certainly reduce the risks by being nosy. Don't be fobbed off by glib protestations or indignation. If the vendor is reluctant to offer tangible confirmation that all is above board, then he may have something to hide.

17 Selling

It occurred to me some years ago that charm schools for hitch-hikers might have merit. I see some of them on the verges, unkempt and bedraggled, cigarettes dangling from their lips, a slovenly thumb jerking me to stop, and two fingers seen in the rear view mirror marking the rejection of their requests. Do they seriously expect me to pick them up? Do they believe that, on appearances at least, I could be persuaded that their company was preferable to solitary hours behind the wheel? Surely their aims are to travel at my expense, so why don't they take the trouble to be attractive?

Whatever the commodity, selling is a form of seduction. And the seducee always has the option to say 'no' if what's being offered doesn't appeal. Although this is a blindingly obvious truth, most hitch-hikers and some yachtsmen have yet to learn it.

Just recently, an overseas client was interested in a largish sailing boat. Before going to the expense of air fares, he asked me to have a preliminary look at it. From the outside it appeared fairly impressive, but when I went below my heart sank. Mouldering food remained in the galley lockers; unwashed plates lay in the sink; personal clothing was strewn in grubby clumps about the cabin; a festering brown lump was identified as a tea bag. I was certain the boat had stood unattended since the end of the previous season, although the 'Owner's Comments' on the brokerage details gushed 'a lovingly maintained family yacht, ready to put to sea at once!'.

Understandably, my client was not impressed when I reported to him. A meticulous man, he reasoned that if the owner couldn't be bothered to keep it clean, what chance was there that the rest of boat had been properly cared for?

The boat — its own shop window: First impressions are vital. The boat business is dream business and dreams are fragile things. The potential purchaser imagines himself at the helm of some trim and tidy craft, cleaving the waters with immaculate bows; not at sea in something resembling a floating garbage skip. If, when he boards, he is instantly repelled, it will be an uphill struggle from then on to convince him that beneath the grime lies quality.

And imagine any future surveys. Surveyors try hard to be objective, but even they are influenced by involuntary reactions. Personally, although I can stand any amount of clutter at home, the sight of a badly kept yacht makes me smoulder with outrage; and doubtless my disappointment threads through my reports. A comment such as 'a sound and obviously well maintained vessel' will probably encourage a buyer. But less enthusiasm — 'although generally sound, this vessel shows signs of considerable neglect' — would be likely to have the opposite effect.

A tidy, well presented boat will not only be easier to sell, but will also command a higher price. It is very much in the seller's interest to display what is, after all, the 'bait' in as tempting a manner as possible.

Gilding an honest lily: But, whereas tidying up a boat for sale is one thing; disguising her as something she isn't is quite another.

Disappointment is profoundly damping. For the buyer to discover that the bird of paradise is actually a turkey, is likely to seriously turn him off. For example, to fleetingly restore the shine of gelcoat, well weathered beyond any superficial restoration, is a deception which will probably rebound. Even if the buyer doesn't see though it (quite literally), the surveyor certainly will.

It's better by far to present the boat honestly, and to offer it at a price which is appropriate to its condition, than to tart it up, hopeful that someone more gullible than yourself will come along. Word travels fast in boating circles. The risk of being rumbled is high.

So, declare all known defects: A man I knew had a handsome GRP sailing yacht which he had owned since new, and on which he had lavished great care. When the boat was ten years old his insurance company asked for a survey. I was instructed to do this.

'Nice boat', I told him over the phone. 'But there are a few blisters.'

I could almost hear him go pale at the other end. 'What's that?' he stammered. 'Not...not...osmosis?'

I told him that this indeed was the case, and reassured him

111

that it wasn't severe and could be satisfactorily treated. He seemed deeply troubled at the news — almost reluctant to discuss the matter at any length.

Less than a week later I was surprised to see a 'For Sale' sign dangling from the pulpit. From another source I heard that the price was very keen indeed. And, as this was an exceptionally attractive boat, it wasn't long before the owner was holding a deposit and another surveyor was crawling over her.

'It was those bloody blisters,' the owner told me later. 'I though I had it all wrapped up, but the osmosis scared him off.' And away he trudged, paintbrush in hand, to touch up the patches of antifouling the surveyor had removed.

Apparently, three more interested parties came and went before he again appeared in my office. 'I'll just have to reduce the price again,' he groaned. 'I've dropped it twice already. By heavens, you'd think it was the deal of the century as it is.'

'Are you telling them?', I asked.

The owner looked appalled. 'About the osmosis? Good God, no! They'd run a mile!'

Several cups of coffee later I had persuaded him not to reduce the price at all but, instead, to actually *raise* it back to the original, and perfectly fair sum he wanted. Less easily, I also managed to convince him that not everyone was as nervous about osmosis as he seemed to be. My advice was that he should make it plain to all comers that the defect was known, and that a cash allowance for this had already been made.

A few days later he sold the boat.

The moral of this story is clear. For the purchaser, unexpected news is usually bad news. If he's sufficiently rattled, he could easily be frightened off altogether. At the very least he'll be provoked into a flurry of hostile bargaining, from which you, the vendor, will certainly emerge the loser.

I believe it is always better to be totally candid about the condition of your boat. If a defect is known it should be declared from the outset. Not only will you impress a potential buyer with your honesty, but you will effectively remove these issues from the bargaining table.

The inventory — little things mean a lot: Ideally, boats should be displayed for sale with every included item aboard — and nothing more. But this is sometimes impracticable. Boats often change hands whilst still in commission, when they will obviously also be carrying personal gear which will be removed at some time. And, if laid up ashore, valuable equipment — sails, dinghy, navigational instruments, et cetera — may have been taken off for security.

The alternative is a written inventory in which *every* item of portable equipment is specified. For the buyer to learn later that the barometer he thought he had bought along with the boat was actually a cherished gift from your late Uncle Fred (and is now only a discoloured patch on the bulkhead) is to invite contention. A detailed list will head off any argument.

But make sure this list is truly comprehensive. Unquantified descriptions such as 'sundry deck gear' won't do. A friend of mine sailed his recently acquired cruiser round from Plymouth. With it snugly attached to his mooring way out in Poole Bay, he pumped up the dinghy eager to row ashore — and then discovered that he had no oars!

Brokerage or private?: This is the sellers' recurrent dilemma. Should you handle all the advertising and other negotiations yourself, or would it be better to place your boat in the hands of a yacht broker to take advantage of his knowledge and promotional skills?

Most professional yacht brokers in the UK belong to the *Association of Brokers and Yacht Agents* (known as ABYA) and the *Yacht Brokers, Designers, and Surveyors Association* (YBDSA), who lay down qualifications for membership and require their members to abide by a strict Code of Practice.

British yacht brokers charge commission, usually at a rate of 8% of the final price, on a 'no sale — no fee' basis. Obviously this can be a a very hefty sum — £800 on a £10,000 deal — which, if you decided to go it alone, could either be saved for yourself or knocked off the asking price to give you a competitive edge against other boats on the market.

However, there are some distinct advantages in letting a broker handle the sale. Amongst these are:

1) The exposure your yacht will get. Most brokers use prominent display boards outside their offices, and take regular advertising space in the various sailing magazines. Even if your

boat isn't advertised specifically, these ads will attract general enquiries which could lead towards a sale.

2) The yacht broker should be available to deal with enquiries at any reasonable time, on any day of the week. If you're chained to a desk during working hours, or live some distance from where your boat is kept, this could be an important consideration.

3) The broker will act as an intermediary on your behalf. Some people find face-to-face negotiations awkward, or feel that they could handle them better if someone else was acting as their spokesman.

4) The broker will deal with all the 'business' for you — the sales agreement, holding the deposit, and the final transfer of title. He can introduce the buyer to advantageous sources of finance, and help him with insurance. Obviously, the easier you make it for the buyer, the better the chance of making a sale.

The hypoactive yacht broker: Although by far the majority of yacht brokers are conscientious and professional, unfortunately some are not.

Occasionally you will come across one who sees himself as hardly more than a key-holder — 'Here are the details, sir. She's up in the saltings at the head of Bloodshot Creek. I'd show you over her, but it looks like rain and I'm expecting an important overseas 'phone call. If you'd like to make an offer, I should still be here when you get back. If not, I'll be having a swift half down at the Muddled Duck'... And so on.

Quite clearly such a man would be about as useful to you as a bottomless bailer. But, if you feel like supporting him as an act of charity, it may be less frustrating simply to give him his commission at once and then sell the boat yourself.

The dual approach: Of course there's no reason why you shouldn't list your boat with the brokers whilst concurrently trying to sell it yourself. Classified advertisements placed in the appropriate magazines, details pinned to yacht club notice boards, and the jungle drums of local gossip could all yield fruitful enquiries.

But be sure to offer the boat at the same price everywhere. No broker is going to be encouraged to toil on your behalf if he sees it advertised, discounted by his commission. What you subsequently knock off when face to face with a potential buyer would, of course, be entirely up to you.

And finally: So, there you are. You bought a boat and now you have sold it. What now? Well, unless the whole experience turned you off completely you will probably buy another some day soon. Unlike measles, a single bout of boating brings no immunity from further attacks. Statistically, you are highly likely to relapse.

As a man once said to me as he walked into my office: 'I'm not sure whether I need a surveyor or a psychiatrist — but, while I'm deciding, there's this nifty little ketch I would like you to have a look at for me.'

Index

abrasion, gelcoat, 49
aft cabin, 27
alloy mast, 71
aluminium,
    construction, 30
anchor, 84
Association of Brokers and
    Yacht Agents (ABYA),
    14, 113
auxiliary, engine, 90

bareboat charter, 23
batten, 82
battery, 96
berth, 26
bilge keel, 11, 27
blister, 53
Boat Mart International, 20
boat pox, 52
breasthook, 46
broker, 14, 33
brokerage, 102, 113
Bruce, anchor, 84

camera, 33
carvel, 37
    splined, 37
caulking, 40
centre cockpit, 27
chafe, sail, 82
chain plate, 75
chined hull, 37
Classic Boat, 20
classified advertisement, 17
cleat, 86
clencher, 37
clevis pin, 79

clinker, 37
cold moulded, 37
Coniophora Puteana, 43
construction, 29
cooker, 100
core separation, deck, 62
corrosion, 72
CQR, anchor, 84
crazing, gelcoat, 50
    star, 50
    stress, 56
crevice corrosion, 92
crew register, 23
cutless bearing, 94
cutter, 28

Danforth, anchor, 84
Decca, 99
deck beam, 46
deck, GRP, 61
delamination, 38, 50
Delta, anchor, 84
diesel, engine, 88
dry rot, 43

echo-sounder, 99
electrochemical softening,
    wood, 42
engine, 88
    bearer, 90
    mount, 90
eye, wire, 77

fading, gelcoat, 49
fastening, 40, 46
ferro-cement, 31
ferro-concrete, 31
ferrule, 77
fibre aligned blister, 54
fin keel, 28
flotilla holiday, 23

frame, 44
fuel tank, 91

galvanic corrosion, 31
galvanised wire rope, 77
gas installation, 100
gelcoat, 49
   crazing, 50
   peeling, 55
   thinning, 50
glass reinforced plastic
   (GRP), 29, 49
grain pin, 47
grit-blasting, 55
guardwire, 77, 85

halyard, 77, 79
hanging knee, 46
hatch, 87
hogging, hull, 38
hull, 52
hull/deck joint, 65

injection pump, 89
injector, 89
inventory, 113

keel, 27
ketch, 28

laid deck, 47
lapstrake, 37
lodging knee, 46

magazine, 18
marine borer, 38
   glue, 47
maritime lien, 109
mast, 28, 70
   step, 75
   alloy, 71

masthead sheave, 74
Merchant Shipping
   Act, 108
moisture meter, 35
Motor Boat &
   Yachting, 20
Motor Boats
   Monthly, 20
multihull, 28
Multihull International, 19

Norseman, 77

osmosis, 52
   treatment, 55
ownership, proof of, 108

P strut, 94
pad eye, 72
paint, 51
pipeline, 91
planing hull, 58
plating, steel, 66
plywood, deck, 46
polyester, 79
polypropylene, 80
Port of Registry, 108
possessory lien, 109
power boat, 58
Practical Boat
   Owner, 20
price limit, 16
prop shaft, 92
propeller, 90, 91
pulpit, 85

reefing, 83
rigging, 70
   screw, 79
roller reef, 83
rope, 79

rot, 38
   dry, 43
   wet, 43
rudder, 60
   skeg, 59
   stock, 61
running backstay, 77
running cost, 25
rust, 68
   weep, 42

sagging, hull, 38
sailcloth weight, 82
sails, 81
sales agreement, 102
   deposit, 102
schooner, 28
seam, 38
Serpula Lachrymans, 43
shaft alignment, 94
sheave, 74
sheet, 79
sheet plywood,
   construction, 37
skeg, 59
sloop, 28
Small Ships Register, 108
solid plank, deck, 47
spar, 70
   timber, 71
splined carvel, 37
split ring, 79
   seam, 40
spray rail, 58
spreader, 72, 73
Sta-Lok, 77
stainless steel wire, 77
stanchion, 85
standing rigging, 77
star crazing, 50
statutory lien, 109

steel, 66
   construction, 30
stern drive, 94
stock, rudder, 61
stress crazing, 56
strip plank, 37
survey, 103
surveyor, 33, 103
swage, 77

Talurit, 77
tang, 72
teak clad deck, 48
teak on GRP, deck, 63
teak on ply, deck, 46
thinning gelcoat, 50
timber spar, 71
transverse floor, 46
trial sail, 21
trim tab, 95

ultrasonic gauge, 69
upholstery, 99
UV resistant
   sailcloth, 92

weld, 66
wet rot, 43
wicking, 54
   treatment, 55
winch, 86
windlass, 86
wire rope, 76
wiring, 97
wood –
   modern technique,
   construction, 30
wood –
   traditional,
   construction, 29
wrung, hull, 38

Yacht Brokers and
    Designers and Surveyors
    Association (YBDSA), 15,
    104, 113
Yachting Monthly, 19
Yachting World, 19
Yachts and Yachting, 19
yawl, 28

Useful Addresses

Andrew Simpson & Associates
Davis's Boatyard, Cobb's Quay,
Hamworthy, Poole, Dorset, BH15 4EJ
Tel: (0202) 670754 or (0860) 433163
Fax: (0202) 671705

British Marine Industries Federation
Meadlake Place, Thorpe Lea Road,
Egham, Surrey, TW20 8HE
Tel: (0784) 473377
Fax: (0784) 439678

Cruising Association
Ivory House, St. Katherine's Dock,
London, E1 9AT
Tel: (071) 481 0881

Registrar of British Shipping
HM Customs and Excise,
Portcullis House,
21 Cowbridge Road East,
Cardiff, CF1 9SS
Tel: (0222) 238531. Ext 4143
Note: Addresses of all other registry
ports may be obtained here.

Royal Yachting Association
RYA House, Romsey Road,
Eastleigh, Hants, SO5 4YA
Tel: (0703) 629962

Small Ships Registry
DVLA, Swansea, SA99 1BX
Tel: (0702) 783355

Yacht Brokers, Designers & Surveyors Assoc.
Wheel House, Petersfield Road,
White Hill, Bordon, Hants, GU35 9BU
Tel: (0420) 473862
Fax: (0420) 488328

DIVINE ENERGY

THE ORTHODOX PATH TO CHRISTIAN VICTORY

JON E. BRAUN

CONCILIAR PRESS
Ben Lomond, California

DIVINE ENERGY
©1991 Jon E. Braun
All rights reserved
Printed in the United States of America

Conciliar Press
P.O. Box 76, Ben Lomond, California 95005-0076

Library of Congress Cataloging in Publication Data

Braun, Jon E.
    Divine energy: the Orthodox path to Christian victory / Jon E. Braun
        p. cm.
    ISBN 0-9622713-1-4 : $8.95
    1. Spiritual life--Orthodox Eastern authors.
    2. Spiritual warfare.
    3. Orthodox Eastern Church--Doctrines.
    4. Braun, Jon E.
    I. Title.
    BX382.B73   1991
    248.4'819--dc20   91-21264
                                                      CIP